PRAISE FOR *THE GOSPEL ARC*

"Hatton's work offers ministers a way to offer winsome witness to the Living Word through the Written Word. This book will help 'those who have a fire caught up in their bones' to declare more faithfully and fruitfully the crucified, risen, reigning, and returning Lord, who calls all people in all places to follow the arc of his life and love."
—TODD D. STILL, dean, Truett Theological Seminary

"With keen insight and great inspiration, Hatton shows us the life-giving necessity for the preacher to encounter Jesus himself through the study of Scripture. *The Gospel Arc* provides preachers with an effective tool that ably advises how to preach the biblical text in light of Jesus' work even as this text provides our understanding of who Jesus is. . . . A true gift to preachers and Christian communicators alike."
—PREBEN VANG, director, Doctor of Ministry program, Truett Theological Seminary

"This book shows how to preach Christ through all the Scriptures. It is well organized, carefully presented, and biblically sound. I am thrilled to recommend it, offering the prayer that this helpful guide will lead us afresh to Christ and that he would become the focal point of a kind of Christian preaching that is sound, relevant, motivating, and life-changing."
—JOHN D. HANNAH, professor, Dallas Theological Seminary

"*The Gospel Arc* is not a how-to manual for becoming a better preacher/pastor; it is a method of discovering Jesus and his salvation in the text! . . . Jeff is one of the greatest preachers I have ever sat under and I cannot recommend this book enough. It is not only helpful for preachers caught in the weekly grind of coming up with 'fresh' sermons, but it will help you devotionally to see and discover Jesus in ways that enliven your soul."
—PETE HATTON, pastor, Redeemer Edmond, Edmond, Oklahoma

"*The Gospel Arc* follows the rich tradition of great books on preaching. Here Dr. Hatton illuminates two important poles of exposition—the historical context and the eternal meaning of Christ and his salvation. Hatton bridges these two poles to return Christ through the Word and Spirit to the forefront of the sermon. A practical and refreshing guide, this enlightening book underscores having Jesus at the forefront of biblical exposition. This book will surely transform both the messengers and hearers of God's Word."

—BILL THOMAS, executive director, SW Church Planting Network

"As a college student, the gospel came alive to me in new ways through Jeff Hatton's preaching, and I was energized to learn to preach Christ myself.... I am thrilled this material is now in book form and I trust it will encourage and equip preachers to proclaim Jesus and his salvation from every text of the Bible. I know it is giving me a fresh wave of desire to encounter Jesus in the text!"

—DAVID RAPP, pastor, Redeemer Presbyterian Church, Temple, Texas

"*The Gospel Arc* shows us how to 'take Jesus with us' as we read and preach Scripture. After twenty-two years of preaching to the same congregation, Jeff Hatton shows us how to use contemporary, yet really ancient, tools in order to participate with the Lord in the preaching of him from our hearts and from all of Scripture."

—JOSEPH RYAN, former chancellor, Redeemer Seminary, Dallas

"Jeff Hatton has a lot of experience in ministry. But, as I know, a lot of experience golfing doesn't help unless you have the right swing. Jeff does. Actually, it's an arc: the greatest story ever told, because it is about the Father's saving mercy in Christ from Genesis to Revelation. But how do you 'preach Christ' from the whole Bible? Jeff shows us how to connect the text in its original context to the wider scope of the unfolding story. If we're looking for real transformation in our lives, churches, and communities, it starts right where this book directs us."

—MICHAEL HORTON, professor, Westminster Seminary California

The Gospel Arc

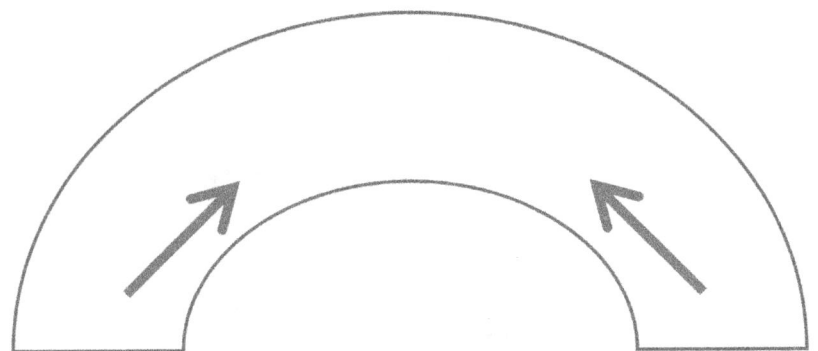

The Gospel Arc

Preaching that Experiences Jesus with the Bible

JEFF HATTON

WIPF & STOCK · Eugene, Oregon

THE GOSPEL ARC
Preaching that Experiences Jesus with the Bible

Copyright © 2021 Jeff Hatton. All rights reserved. Except for brief quotations in critical publications or reviews, no part of this book may be reproduced in any manner without prior written permission from the publisher. Write: Permissions, Wipf and Stock Publishers, 199 W. 8th Ave., Suite 3, Eugene, OR 97401.

Wipf & Stock
An Imprint of Wipf and Stock Publishers
199 W. 8th Ave., Suite 3
Eugene, OR 97401

www.wipfandstock.com

PAPERBACK ISBN: 978-1-7252-7062-6
HARDCOVER ISBN: 978-1-7252-7063-3
EBOOK ISBN: 978-1-7252-7064-0

05/04/21

Contents

Acknowledgments ix
Preface xi

PART 1: WHY THE GOSPEL ARC?
Chapter 1   Leaving Jesus Behind 3
Chapter 2   Leaving Jesus Behind in Preaching 12

PART 2: THE GOSPEL ARC
Chapter 3   Introducing the Gospel Arc 21
Chapter 4   The Gospel Arc Preaching Manual 27

PART 3: DOING THE GOSPEL ARC
Chapter 5   Listen to the Text 39
Chapter 6   Understand the Text 46
Chapter 7   Discover the Text's Message 56
Chapter 8   Discover the Textual Jesus 67
Chapter 9   Craft a Sermon Message 82

PART 4: THE BIBLICAL-THEOLOGICAL POWER OF THE GOSPEL ARC
Chapter 10   The Power of Listening to the Text 95
Chapter 11   The Power of Understanding the Text ... 104
Chapter 12   The Power of Discovering the Text's Message ... 107
Chapter 13   The Power of Discovering the Textual Jesus ... 121
Chapter 14   The Power of Crafting a Sermon Message ... 142

Appendix A: The Gospel Arc Preaching Manual 147
Appendix B: A Sample Week with the Gospel Arc Preaching Manual 157
Appendix C: A Sermon Transcript of Romans 10:1–4 159
Bibliography 163
Subject Index 167
Name Index 171
Scripture Index 173

Acknowledgments

I am thankful for my ministry mentors and friends over the years. John Hannah for introducing me to the revolutionary idea that the gospel is for Christians too. And for befriending me. Paul Settle for patiently walking me through the doctrines of grace. Joseph "Skip" Ryan for being my pastor and embodying extravagant grace. They are champions for experiencing Jesus and his salvation with the Bible for all of life and ministry.

I am thankful to the congregation of Redeemer Presbyterian Church, Waco, Texas for their loyal friendship and dogged passion to move the Gospel Arc Preaching model beyond Waco. They have loved and encouraged me through the many challenges of planting an old school "parachute drop" church plant and then anchoring a gospel church in Waco. We are a gosepl team learning to build our messy lives, relationships, and ministry around Jesus and his salvation. It is a joy and honor to do life together, and to make friends and have gospel conversations with as many people as possible in Waco.

I am thankful to my friends at Truett Seminary. Todd Still for his friendship and guidance in this preaching project become book, which were invaluable. He understood what I was trying to do better than I did and set me on a path that was a lamp unto my feet. He turned the phrase that captures the heart of the Gospel Arc, "Those who preach with him in view encounter him anew," because he does. Preben Vang for pastoring me. It comes naturally to him. His firm vision for my success and his self-giving leadership to get me there was priceless. Thank you, both.

I am thankful for my parents, Chris and Jean Hatton, and my brother, Pete Hatton. My first family and life-long cheerleaders of all things Jeff Hatton. They are the unrelenting presence of loyal love to me. Words fail. . .

My children Cal, Bryn, Knox, Belle, and Ty. Truth be told, I beg God to make me a gospel preacher for their sake—so that Jesus would shine on the page for them. Routinely every summer vacation I ask, "What do y'all want me to preach on this year?" We have been gospel teammates from the beginning. My love for them. . .well, it often overwhelms me.

Speaking of, I am overwhelmed with gratitude and love for my wife, Nancy Hatton. Nancy has been my greatest cheerleader, friend, confidant, comforter, help, strength, teammate, and warrior. Ministry has the unique ability to crush you, your marriage, and your family. Often you feel outnumbered and surrounded. Hermione's words to Harry before his inevitable doom at the hands of Lord Voldemort are Nancy's, "I will go with you." Perhaps even more heroic, she has the distinct call of being married to a difficult man and makes it look easy. She is a warrior-princess. I love you honey.

Preface

If you throw a brick into a pack of dogs, the one that yelps is the one you hit.

—Dr. John Hannah

Dr. Hannah spoke these words to me after a church history class my first semester in seminary. I responded in disbelief, "Are you calling me a dog?"

A year before I spoke with Dr. Hannah, I was in the middle of an evangelistic conversation in Wildwood, New Jersey. I found myself on a beach with a group of inebriated and half-dressed twenty-somethings. I was talking to them about their need for Jesus and his salvation when an intrusive thought burst into my brain, "Why do I need Jesus, as a Christian?" Unlike most of the questions, these twenty-somethings asked about the Bible being true, the nature of truth, other religions, and the uniqueness of Christianity. I was at a loss to answer this one. It rattled me. Eventually our conversation wrapped up, and I began a long walk back, talking out loud to myself the entire way.

"Do I only need Jesus for divine enablement to somehow *do* the Christian life and ministry, kind of like Luke Skywalker needed the Force?" I asked. "If the force is with me, I'm good to go. If not, I'm toast?" I reasoned. Perhaps I could have survived my spiritual spiral with an affirmative, "Yes! Jesus is my Force. Now back to ministry!" But I could not do it. Deeper magic was at work.

"Ok, so it all comes down to the need to activate God in my life and ministry . . . well, how do you do that?" Even as I rehearsed this all too familiar understanding of my "need" for Jesus, I knew it was a dead end. The school of experience over the years had been an inflexible teacher—activating God simply did not work. And the endless effort was ruining me.

I could not figure out how Jesus avoided being a "rear-view mirror Jesus." Someone, I needed to become a Christian but then functionally left behind to live the Christian life. No one drives their car looking through the rear-view mirror at the road behind them, right? So it's the front windshield that is non-negotiable, but that seemingly simple choice comes with endless options: surrenders, secrets, formulas, disciplines, techniques, principles, laws, how to's, passion, devotion, five-hundred page discipleship manuals, tapping into the Holy Spirit, imitating dead spiritual giants, small groups, and more to activate God in your life depending upon one's tradition, theological stripe, personality, and the ever sacred personal experience.

"Or maybe," I thought with resignation, "Jesus is simply the ultimate friend who never leaves you, and he just so happens to be God, too." My "need" then would be purely relational, emotional, psychological. On and on and on it went. I told you it was a long walk back.

I was no stranger to ministry up to this point. I had logged seven years of campus ministry. Seven years of sharing the gospel to skeptics in the Ivy League: Brown University and Harvard University. Not to mention my time on the other side of the world starting the first campus ministries in Alma-Alta, Kazakhstan and Bishkek, Kirghizstan. Despite being on the front lines of watching God at work among a variety of students all over the world, I was exhausted.

It was not the good kind of exhaustion that Jesus talks about from an over-abundance of ministry amidst the need for more workers (Matt 9:37). It was the kind of exhaustion that breaks you down at the roots of your being. No matter how hard I tried, I could not shake it.

I tried spiritual disciplines, effective ministry practices, different theologies, and traditions of life change. Then I tried various spiritual secrets and techniques. I listened endlessly to the teaching of favorite pastors, speakers, and best-sellers—again and again. I researched multiple views on the ministry of the Holy Spirit and biblical principles that "worked" for others. For a while even, I thought life and ministry were about the "it factor." You simply had "it" or you did not. If you did, you were one of the lucky ones who survived, and maybe if you were *really* lucky, you thrived. I tried it all.

Nothing worked. I was not getting better. I felt myself getting worse. And more desperate. Perhaps you can relate.

So here I was, sitting in Dr. Hannah's class that first semester of seminary. I was burned-out before it was popular and disillusioned with chasing the "next thing." But Dr. Hannah's free and frequent use of the "gospel" was somehow energizing. He went beyond my reductionistic and self-activating notions of the gospel into a whole new grammar of the gospel that started working on me. He would describe the gospel as something immediately relevant for the Christian, even pastors. Strangely, the gospel began to reach those exhausted roots of my being. One day, I went up to him after class, "Dr. Hannah, you keep talking about the gospel—gospel, gospel, gospel— what are you talking about? Are you talking about evangelism?"

What he said next hit me, well, like a brick. He looked at me sideways, in the way he does, and said, "Jeff, the gospel is not something you *do*. It is something Jesus has *done* for you, outside of you. And what he has done reaches and renews not only the unbelieving person, but also the believing . . . even pastors." A gospel revolution began in my life, relationships, and ministry.

A dominating aspect of this gospel revolution in my life has been an obsession with preaching Jesus and his salvation in all the Bible (Genesis to Revelation). My obsession is not with a "UFO Jesus" entering the airspace of the text like an unidentified flying object that no one sees coming—not the text nor even God himself! In other words, "UFO Jesus" floats high above the text in one's imagination, landing nowhere.

Nor is my obsession with a "Systematic Jesus" who saves the sermon with theological accuracy, but is textually and, thereby, personally irrelevant and impotent. In other words, "Systematic Jesus" is a shallow, repetitive, abstract, and boring Jesus who informs, not transforms.

My obsession, perhaps most of all, is not with the most popular Jesus of all— "Pelagian Jesus," the ultimate "Fixer-Upper." Pelagian-Jesus saves the world by the power of self-improvement. He tells us how to fix our lives, relationships, and the world from the blueprint of the Bible. Really good, convincing stuff. Each biblical text is loaded with possibilities to activate God in your life, relationships, and the world. There are challenging moral standards, itemized biblical principles, endless studies in character, enlightened spiritual techniques, secret access points to the Holy Spirit, transferable spiritual experiences, and discipleship material for the fully devoted to mention a few.

Nope. My obsession has been for a "Textual Jesus" in all the Bible. A "Textual Jesus" who shows up in THAT text with a specific aspect of his person and work to reach and renew me and the world. A "Textual Jesus" to be experienced by faith with the Bible, thereby, changing everything. Is there such a Jesus in the Bible?

The longer I live with myself, the more aware I am of my primal struggle to be my own savior *and* (introducing a counter present power) the healing power of Jesus' gracious love for me. My need to perform has finally met its match. The good news of Jesus Christ and his comprehensive salvation reaches and renews lives, homes, relationships, pastors, churches, neighborhoods, communities, all kinds of places, and the culture. The gospel—good news, not good advice—changes everything. Therefore, experiencing Jesus with the Bible is immediately relevant in any culture at any time. It is the normal, everyday, work of the Holy Spirit in any life and community—in mine and in yours.

The Gospel Arc is all about the need for both the preacher and hearer to experience Jesus with the Bible by faith. It arises out of my own exhausting school of experience and primal need for Jesus and his salvation in all of life and ministry. It became my obsession when the grammar of the gospel began to hit me, well, like a brick through the teaching of Dr. John Hannah. It became my passion to preach the personal active presence of Jesus and his salvation in all the Bible, and to help others do the same. It became the energetic focus of some doctoral work to practically help preaching that experiences Jesus with the Bible. I am excited here to share the Gospel Arc to inspire preachers to experience Jesus with the Bible, with a particular focus on preparing (crafting) and proclaiming (delivering) the sermon. Perhaps, you are transformed in the process. Perhaps God uses you to reach your hearers in a new way. Perhaps a gospel revolution breaks out. Taking Jesus with you changes everything.

PART 1

Why the Gospel Arc?

Chapter 1

Leaving Jesus Behind

THIS IS US

Every parent's nightmare comes true in the second chapter of Luke's gospel. After unknowingly leaving Jerusalem without their twelve-year-old boy, Mary and Joseph find themselves a day away from Jerusalem with no Jesus in sight (Luke 2:41–51). Of course they freak out! "Where is Jesus?!" Leaving Jesus behind is devastating for Mary and Joseph. Leaving Jesus behind is devastating for all of us.

In fact, leaving Jesus behind is the broken pattern of *every* human heart, Christian or not. It is inherent to our collapsed nature—it is quintessentially us—we leave Jesus behind. And it is not simply about "moral failure" or a constant sin struggle; it is not a lack of surrender to God and his will for your life; and it certainly is not the failure to apply a list of biblical principles or to tap into the mysterious movements of the Holy Spirit.

Leaving Jesus behind is the obsession to be one's own savior.[1] It is the universal broken need to be more than human, that is, godlike (Gen 3).

---

1. Anglican priest Johnny Sertin diagnoses the overall empty spiritual state of the church in England as that of "leaving Jesus behind" and emphasizes the Western church's need to experience many mini-resurrections from "the death of leaving Jesus behind." From Sertin's discussion, "Sharing the Kingdom 7340."

We struggle to attain that ever-elusive righteousness, the justification of our very being. We fear condemnation, the doom or nothingness of our existence. Therefore, we search for salvation everywhere, in anything and anyone. We must have a savior.

Strangely, the myth of control remains intact throughout our anxious and exhausting quest to be more. We refuse to give up thinking, feeling, willing, trusting, relating, doing, and living like we have the ability to bear the burden of saviorhood. Leaving Jesus behind is the normal human condition. It is so woven into the very fabric of our being that it is simply our nature. Leaving Jesus behind lives in our DNA.

"If you want to understand what makes someone tick, or why they're behaving the way they are, trace the righteousness in play, and things will likely become clear."[2] The obsession to save ourselves explains us—it is our grasp for control, to feel "righteous," be enough, find cosmic love and acceptance, or avoid doom, that is, the death of our very being. That deep sense that we are not enough and dreadfully unable to do anything about it, reveals us to us. It is our inner drama. The anxiety of nothingness is real.

Therefore, leaving Jesus behind is the radical diagnosis of the human condition in all its multi-forms of self-imprisonment. It is who we are and what we do apart from the divine intrusion of Jesus and his salvation. The Apostles were no exception; neither are Christians.

PETER LEAVES JESUS BEHIND

Many of the Galatian Christians were racists because they refused to associate themselves with the Gentile Christians.[3] They created divisions between what they saw as "pure" and "impure" Christianity. The Galatian Christians with ties to Judaism and the law saw themselves as spiritually superior and privileged in comparison to the Gentile Galatian Christians.[4]

---

2. Zahl, *Seculosity*, iv.

3. In light of today's struggle to define racism, I am defining it *vertically*, that is, with reference to one's relationship (or lack of relationship) to Jesus and his achieved righteousness for the unrighteous (Romans 4.5). In other words, whenever race is the source (formally or functionally) of an individual's or group's identity, justification, righteousness, sense of worth and value, or love and acceptance *before* God, others, themselves, the traditional law (i.e., the ten commandments), a spiritually progressive law (i.e., the "quiet time"), or the endless little laws of life (i.e., the law of thinness or racial superiority), then a line is drawn between "us" and "them." Inclusion and exclusion inescapably act out based upon the identity marker or form of righteousness, regardless of one's perspective of Paul. Therefore, racism is a works-based-identity not a grace-based-identity. It is a race-identity not a Jesus-identity.

4. Irrespective of one's perspective of Paul, our functional justification or

In other words, to be a Jewish Christian in Galatia meant that you were *more* than the others. In Galatia, your functional righteousness or acceptance before God and one another was earned by a mixture of Jesus, race, and law-keeping. Peter, an Apostle and pillar of the church in Galatia, was no exception. Peter left Jesus behind. He left the thick righteousness of Jesus for the thin veil of his own, namely, his race and its national laws. He left a received-righteousness by grace for a self-attained righteousness by works, thereby "turning to a different gospel" (Gal 1.6). Peter was struggling to attain that ever-elusive righteousness, the justification of his very being. The obsession to be his own savior was real.

Paul saw Peter's racism as abhorrent, but he was even more disturbed by Peter's *reason* for being racist: he left Jesus behind. Paul saw that Peter believed in Jesus and his salvation (the gospel) at one level and yet did not at far deeper levels in his life.[5] Even a pillar apostle had "un-evangelized" areas of his life—areas where Jesus and his salvation had not yet gone—areas where he was determined to be his own functional savior regardless of his formal beliefs. Peter left Jesus behind.[6]

Theologically speaking, Peter left Jesus behind by relying upon a works-salvation instead of a grace-salvation for his functional righteousness, identity, or love and acceptance before God, others, himself, the law (moral law), any progressive spiritual laws, and the endless "little laws" of life like thinness, capability, or success.[7]

But it did not stop there for Peter and it does not stop there for us. When we leave Jesus behind for our functional identity (justification), it corrupts our pursuit of the Christian life (sanctification). In other words, leaving Jesus behind in the one (justification) guarantees leaving Jesus behind in the other (sanctification). Therefore, self-justification always leads to self-sanctification doctrinally (formally) and experientially (functionally).

---

righteousness before God, others, ourselves, and the law in all its forms (see footnote 3 above) shapes our identity, thinking and feeling, relationships, handling of things like money, behavior, and ethics. For example, if one's functional righteousness is self-discipline and hard work, then the "undisciplined and lazy other" is generally looked down upon, that is, viewed and potentially treated as less than (functional condemnation). In other words, the "undisciplined and lazy other" is unworthy of love and acceptance—at least not to the level of the "disciplined and hard-working one." Life, sadly, universally confirms this identity or justification ethic.

5. Keller, *Prodigal* God, 115.

6. Obviously, Peter and the Jewish Christians in Galatia were not the only ones in the ancient world caught up in some form of Jewish-righteousness (see Acts 15).

7. For a helpful historical, biblical, and theological walk through of the perspectives of Paul debate, see Michael Horton's book, *Justification*.

That is, to the belief and practice that we activate God in our life, relationships, and ministry. This is what happened to Peter.

The idea of self-sanctification is crucial to grasp. It is any life change strategy that promotes *faith plus something* rather than *faith alone* to renew or sanctify a life. In other words, self-sanctification is anything other than Jesus and his salvation (faith alone) activating sanctification, changing lives, and restoring relationships.

Therefore, self-sanctification does not rely upon the power of the Holy Spirit to work through faith in a finished Jesus-justification to activate the renewal of lives and relationships. Nor does it rely upon the power of the Holy Spirit to work through faith in a definitive Jesus-deliverance from the dark powers of sin, condemnation, death, and ultimate evil to experientially heal lives and relationships. Nor does it rely upon the power of the Holy Spirit to work through faith in an empty grave and resurrected life to energize being who you already are because of salvation.

Self-sanctification does not formally nor functionally believe the gospel. It leaves Jesus behind. It takes Jesus' place in an attempt to activate life change, even if it is with "God's help." Therefore, self-sanctification not only does not work—because it cannot change a life—but it also gets in the way of the Holy Spirit's reaching and renewing work by means of the gospel in individual lives, relationships, and communities.

On the surface, Peter was the model apostle, protecting the purity of the faith by promoting "holiness." In the hidden regions of his heart, however, Peter was resting and relying on what he perceived to be his "right" performance to be functionally loved, righteous, accepted, holy, or blessed before God and others (i.e., being a law-keeping Jewish Christian).

If the Galatian Christians did not participate in this "right" performance in their sanctification, then Peter and his "holy" friends withheld acceptance and relationship from them (racism). In other words, they did not eat with them (Gal 2:12). In this way, Peter's "conduct was not in step with the truth of the gospel" (Gal 2:13).[8]

---

8. The only hope against the power of racism (wherever it is found) is an identity not defined and driven by works, that is, by race. A race-identity cannot save lives, relationships, communities, and the world. It cannot activate social justice. What a race-identity does do is break down everything in its path. The Apostle Paul says: "There is neither Jew nor Greek, there is neither slave nor free, there is no male or female, for you are all one in Christ Jesus" (Gal 3:28). While not denying the realities of race, gender, and culture, Paul obliterates those ways of defining ourselves, that is, of forming an identity. The only thing, *the only thing*, that matters is the classification of whether or not you are in Christ through faith. This is the aim we should strive for if we want to classify the human race. Therefore, only the gospel of Jesus Christ and his salvation heals racism in the human heart, relationships, communities, and the world.

All is well for Peter until Paul dramatically exposes his "holiness" as racism, driven by the obsession to self-justify (Gal 2:11–14). Strikingly, Paul's solution to Peter's racism is not "Stop it!" or "Five Steps to a Racist Free Life." Or even, "Peter, for the love of God, love like the law says!" Paul's solution to Peter's racism was the gospel: "I saw that their *conduct* was not in step with the *truth of the gospel*" (Gal 2:14, emphasis added). Paul's solution to Peter's self-sanctification was the power of a Jesus-justification.

For Paul, the transfer of trust from a self-achieved righteousness to a grace-received righteousness changes everything. It sanctifies. Even Apostles. The Apostle Paul understood Peter's ultimate problem to be that of functionally disbelieving the gospel of Jesus and his salvation, thereby "turning to a different gospel" that has no power to justify much less sanctify (Gal 1:6). In other words, Peter's ultimate problem was leaving Jesus behind.

Paul knew everyone must have a gospel, righteousness, identity, salvation, or savior. The need is inescapable; the obsession is real. Therefore, what Peter needed was a fresh faith in Jesus and his salvation, simultaneously combined with an intelligent understanding of his heart's particular self-salvation strategy (repentance). We need the same solution for the same problem.

We, like Peter, need to be reached and renewed afresh by Jesus and his salvation (the gospel) to functionally displace our self-reliance in all its multi-forms. We, like Peter, need the power of a Jesus-salvation to experientially reach the fundamental layers of our being that are captured by self-salvation. This functional transfer of trust from self to Jesus is the heart of gospel renewal. It is the essence of learning to "deny (yourself) and take up (your) cross and follow (Jesus)" (Matt 16:24; Mark 8:34; Luke 9:23).

The way to change lives is to change what the heart functionally trusts in, thereby changing what the heart functionally loves or worships. Theologian Mike Horton, channeling Luther's view of biblical renewal, says, "the word of God (specifically, the gospel) produces faith, faith produces love, and love produces good works. For Luther, mixing up the order serves no one. God is offended rather than satisfied, the believer has been deceived, and the neighbor is not served."[9] Every human being is and will be in continual need of this kind of gospel renewal until the end of all things. We, like Peter, need to experience Jesus and his salvation with the Bible. Continually.

The gospel is the power of God alone for real heart, life, and relational change. It gives a righteousness from God that is received not achieved (Rom 1:16–17). Therefore, it ends the struggle for righteousness, including the struggle for a righteousness based on one's race! In Jesus' righteousness, all counterfeit identities finally come to a breathtaking end, making us ENOUGH and ONE before God and each other.

9. Horton, *Justification*, 201.

In this traumatic incident with Peter, the Apostle Paul identifies a basic principle or dark power at work in all of us: the obsession to be our own functional savior (Gal 4:9). In other words, the disordered mega-desire (*epiqumia*) in all of us—from Apostle to regular church goer—to leave Jesus behind. It is a universal obsession that takes a multiplicity of forms.

In Peter's case, it took the form of Jesus plus law keeping and race. In other cases, it may be Jesus plus the law of thinness, Jesus plus human approval, Jesus plus home schooling, or Jesus plus some measurable spiritual success. Pastors continually urge their hearers to "be more like David," reach higher levels of devotion and discipleship, apply this and that biblical principle to marriage and parenting, discover spiritual secrets, access spiritual techniques, activate the Holy Spirit by doing this and doing that, or to "preach the gospel daily and, when necessary, use words." Doing any or all of these, however, *without* a clear meaningful connection to faith in Jesus and his salvation *alone* as the power of God to justify *and* to sanctify a life, becomes self-salvation run amok, ultimately ruining lives, relationships, and communities rather than renewing them.

WE LEAVE JESUS BEHIND

Whatever the expression of self-salvation, the obsession to be one's own savior is the primal impulse driving and enslaving the human heart in endless forms of anxiety, exhaustion, depression, and self-imprisonment (Rom 8:15). We naturally leave Jesus behind; it's what we human beings do. It is so fundamental to our identity, relationships, and life experience, we could say it is our "Adamic-Self" (Rom 5–8).

Therefore, the need to experience Jesus and his salvation with the Bible is not only formally rooted in the universal human condition, but also functionally experienced as the primal obsession for a savior. We desperately need a real Savior, not delusional pretenders and counterfeit substitutes.

Furthermore, the need to experience Jesus and his salvation by faith does not change when one becomes a Christian. What changes is one's relationship to God (justification) and sin (definitive deliverance) but not the nature of sin itself. In other words, although there is a realm transfer for the Christian, sin in the singular (original sin) still stubbornly indwells the Christian.[10] Let me explain . . .

Yes, the universal reign and bondage of sin is over for the Christian. Sin's dominion is dethroned for the Christian; it's domination is definitively defeated by Jesus' death and resurrection. Therefore, the zombie apocalypse

---

10. Rutledge, *Crucifixion*, 168.

is over for the Christian! The "zombie," a physically alive but spiritually dead creature, is no more. A new-self has emerged from the tomb with Jesus. The zombie-self in Adam is no more and a new-self in Christ (i.e., the Spirit-self) has begun. This is massively epic, irreversible life change on-the-spot for the Christian!

At the same time, even though the Christian is no longer a zombie (a big deal), the zombie is still attached to the Christian (Rom 7; Gal 5). This means the Christian is a conflicted-self, split-self, or divided-self (Rom 7.14–25). In other words, the zombie (the unregenerate human being) is one person with one nature, whereas the Christian is one person with two natures. Further, the two natures come about by addition: 1) the nature of the flesh or old self located in the periphery "members" of Paul's body metaphor in Romans 7, and 2) *plus the addition* of the Spirit-self or new self in Christ by the Spirit located in the central controlling position of one's "innermost being" according to Paul's same body metaphor in Romans 7.

What does all this mean? It means that the Christian life is experienced as a civil war, not as an endless victory march (Rom 7; Gal 5). The Christian life is marked by struggling with sin, not the absence of it. A Brown student once told me, "Jeff, before I was a Christian life was less complicated." The sin in the Christian still maintains its deathly DNA; it still terrorizes the Christian to the very end.

Ultimately, however, sin's terrorizing of the Christian loses on all fronts. It obviously loses at the end of all things when Jesus' work is finally and fully applied to the Christian in glorification. But sin's terrorizing also loses in the less visible way of God over-ruling "the body of death" to serve the Christian's present sanctification. Specifically, this is the forging of a healthy and healing humility that is ever-aware of one's sinfulness and inability, and ever-dependent upon Jesus and his salvation—all of which, of course, exalts Christ (Rom 7:24).

Therefore, the dominion of sin has changed for the Christian, but the nature of sin has not (Rom 7–8; Gal 5). The sin's nature will only and always seek to take God's place as Lord and Savior, crave control, deal out death, and de-create lives, relationships, and communities.

Sanctification then is more about "progressively realizing that we exist not 'in Adam,' or in ourselves, but are sharers in Christ's life, death, resurrection, and ascension by a marvelous union" than "simply moving from worse to better."[11] The need to experience Jesus and his salvation (the gospel) by faith continues for the Christian as the functional power (dynamic) of sanctification.

---

11. Horton, *Justification*, 221.

It is the gospel that activates sanctification in the life of the Christian, not the Christian via endless self-activating options. The Holy Spirit works through the hearing of the gospel to activate a fresh faith in Jesus and his salvation that sanctifies or works in love. The Spirit sanctifies lives and relationships by connecting to the infinite riches of Jesus and his salvation by faith for the first time, afresh for the millionth time, or in a newly discovered, unevangelized area of life.

Therefore, there is a need for preaching that wrestles with the reality of sin's intractable, indwelling presence in the Christian, and categorically addresses the dynamic of the Christian's conflicted-self. There is a need for preaching that experiences Jesus with the Bible for the Christian. Taking Jesus with you changes everything.

WE NEED TO EXPERIENCE JESUS WITH THE BIBLE

Working off the Apostle Paul in Galatians, Martin Luther also claims that the default mode of the human heart is self-justification and self-sanctification, or simply self-salvation.[12] In his view, leaving Jesus behind is what comes natural to us; it is simply what human beings do apart from God's gracious work in their lives. Therefore, according to Luther, the need to experience Jesus and his salvation with the Bible by faith is immediately relevant.

Richard Lovelace, an expert on the history of individual and corporate gospel renewal, states that "only a fraction of the present body of professing Christians are solidly appropriating the justifying work of Christ in their lives."[13] In other words, there is a need for Jesus Christ and his salvation not just to be known intellectually but also to be experienced. Gospel renewal counteracts the universal fallen impulse to leave Jesus behind, as Lovelace explains:

> They [Christians] see little need for justification, although below the surface of their lives they are deeply guilt-ridden and insecure . . . in their day-to-day existence they rely on their sanctification for justification . . . drawing their assurance of acceptance with God from their sincerity, their past experience of conversion, their recent religious performance or the relative infrequency of their conscious, willful disobedience.[14]

---

12. Luther, *Commentary on Galatians*, xvi–ii.
13. Lovelace, *Dynamics of Spiritual Life*, 101.
14. Lovelace, *Dynamics of Spiritual Life*, 101.

The gospel of Jesus Christ and his salvation must continually reach and renew the un-evangelized or unreached areas of the believer's life (sanctification). Therefore, according to Lovelace, there is a continual need for gospel renewal among ministers, churches, and communities.

Timothy Keller says, "Revival is not a historical curiosity; it is a consistent pattern of how the Holy Spirit works in a community to arrest and counteract the default mode of the human heart. It is surely relevant to ministry in twenty-first-century global cultures, as it is relevant in every culture."[15]

Historically, the language of "revival" is often associated with a shallow emotionalism. According to Lovelace and Keller, however, true revival is experiencing Jesus and his salvation with the Bible by faith in all of life. Experiencing Jesus and his salvation with the Bible by faith is the justifying and sanctifying work of the Holy Spirit in individual lives, the home, relationships, the church, communities, and the world.

Therefore, the Holy Spirit accompanies the preaching of Jesus and his salvation in all of Scripture, producing faith on-the-spot. A faith that justifies the sinner and sanctifies the split-saint. There is a need for preaching that experiences Jesus with the Bible for everyone. Taking Jesus with you in preaching changes everything.

---

15. Keller, *Center Church*, 55.

Chapter 2

Leaving Jesus Behind in Preaching

Preaching Jesus and his salvation in all of Scripture to be personally and corporately experienced by faith seems to be an unknown cure today for lives, relationships, the church, and a culture that leaves Jesus behind. For many, preaching in the church today might best be characterized as an addiction to good advice.

THE CRISIS OF MORALISTIC PREACHING

Moralistic preaching leaves Jesus behind. It avoids Jesus Christ and his salvation both in sermon preparation and proclamation. Moralistic preaching is self-salvation expressing itself in the form of good advice. The fundamental structure of the sermon today in evangelical churches is straightforward: 1) expound the biblical principle in the text, 2) exhort the biblical principle in the text, and 3) support the exposition and exhortation with illustrations and practical applications.

The effect is immediate upon: 1) listeners struggling with the moral directive in the text who feel burdened and guilty and thereby seek to resolve both by trying harder, and 2) listeners not struggling with the moral directive in the text who think, "I'm so glad I'm not like them," thus becoming further entrenched in self-righteousness. Ironically, Jesus is avoided, both in the Bible and in the sermon.

Abraham Kuruvilla, a preaching professor at Dallas Theological Seminary, seems to establish a moralistic approach to preaching in what he calls the "Christiconic interpretation":

> One may say that each pericope of the Bible is actually portraying a facet of Christlikeness, a segment of the image of Christ: what it means to fulfill a particular divine demand in that pericope after the manner of Christ . . . Each pericope depicts a facet of Christlikeness, even the ones that deal with particular characters in Scripture. In other words, to employ the narratives and characters of the OT for ethical purposes, as the text demands in its theology, *is* to preach Christ.[1]

Kuruvilla argues against Christocentric preaching or the kind of preaching sought in the Gospel Arc: "In a nutshell, the biblical arguments for Christocentric preaching are weak. Before proposing a new hermeneutic for seeing Christ in Scripture, the priority of divine demand and the responsibility of human obedience must be established, for these form the foundation of the Christiconic interpretation to be described."[2]

This type of preaching primarily places Christ in all the Scriptures as example rather than Savior. The central message of the Bible in Christiconic preaching is, "Be like Jesus." Christiconic preaching leaves Jesus behind—it is good advice, not good news. Keller highlights the danger of turning the Bible and preaching into ethical expositions and exhortations disconnected from Jesus Christ and his salvation: "you can have all the sound doctrine possible and be fastidiously performing your ethical and religious duties according to biblical principles and have 'no grace in the heart at all.'"[3]

Good advice preaching creates a church culture obsessed with self-salvation that inevitably leads to spiritual breakdown, toxicity of spirit (self-righteousness), missional impotence, and cultural resistance. Many today think they are rejecting God and Christianity when they are simply rejecting moralism.

How did moralistic preaching become so prevalent? The simple answer is moralism is the default mode of the human condition from Genesis 3 onward. We must save ourselves; we must control our lives. We are obsessed with being our own savior. Thus, the proliferation of self-salvation strategies in the world today, or what the Apostle Paul calls "the weak and

---

1. Kuruvilla, *Privilege the Text!*, 265–66.
2. Kuruvilla, *Privilege the Text!*, 252. See pp. 211–69 for Kuruvilla's more detailed critique of Christocentric preaching and his argument for Christiconic preaching.
3. Keller, *Prayer*, 179.

worthless elementary principles of the world" (Gal 4:9). Moralism is simply what comes natural to us.

A more complex answer is moralism's incestuous relationship with rationalism. We crave certainty and control, even in the way we read the Bible. Therefore, when reason comes along promising both with its rationalistic reading of the Bible, it finds a hero's welcome. The consequence of course is anticipated: reason runs amok in our Bible reading. In this way, reason (the lesser authority) displaces revelation (the greater authority) in an epic effort to read and apply the Bible the "right" or "reasonable" way.

Ironically, the grab for greater certainty and control over the Bible results in catastrophic uncertainty and chaos, which strangely makes sense. The struggle for meaning is now up for grabs to whatever "makes sense." Whatever "makes sense" becomes, well, meaningful. This rationalistic approach to the Bible obviously moves biblical meaning in some pretty weird directions. Wooden literalism comes to mind.

The Enlightenment, therefore, with its absolute devotion to reason and science for ultimate meaning, simply poured gasoline on a fire already burning in the human heart, that is, the fire of moralism. George Lindbeck observes that the offspring of the Enlightenment, biblical criticism and pietistic individualism, simply further entrenched a rationalistic hermeneutic in the church with the naïve attempt to "leap back directly into the Bible" with a supposed neutral rational point of view.[4]

Preaching today has become so identified with moralism that it seems impossible to conceive of the one without the other, and therein lies the inherent challenge for preaching today.[5] The identification between preaching and moralism is so fused today that the only perceivable way to stop the culture's resistance to the church is to stop preaching. In one sense, this approach "makes sense" because moralistic preaching is destructive. In another sense, this approach is fundamentally wrong because moralistic preaching is not biblical preaching.

Therefore, biblical preaching may be an unknown cure for moralism in the church, the church's wrecked relationship with culture, and a fundamental divine source for the healing of both. Preaching today needs to break off its adulterous and abusive relationship with moralism and recognize its already established union to the Better Spouse (Rom 7:1–6). Taking Jesus with you in preaching changes everything.

---

4. Lindbeck, *Church in a Postliberal Age*, 72.

5. Preaching in the postmodern Western church today is noticeably declining in practice. The church's response to moralistic preaching in a postmodern culture—shrink preaching's importance and practice—is understandable.

GOOD NEWS, NOT GOOD ADVICE

Preaching that reaches and renews individuals, preachers, the home, relationships, the church, communities, and the culture proclaims good news, not good advice. Where is God? Where is God at work in people's lives, the church, and the world? Where does one find God? Where does God find individuals and communities? How is the personal, active presence of God released into individual lives, relationships, the church, and the world? The most fundamental answer, according to the Bible, is by hearing good news:

> How then will they call on him in whom they have not believed? And how are they to believe in him of whom they have never heard? And how are they to hear without someone preaching? And how are they to preach unless they are sent? As it is written, "How beautiful are the feet of those who preach the good news!" But they have not all obeyed the gospel. For Isaiah says, "Lord, who has believed what he has heard from us?" So faith comes from hearing, and hearing through the word of Christ. (Rom 10:14–17)

There is an unbridgeable difference between moralistic good advice and biblical good news. According to Tim Keller: "Advice is counsel about what you must do. News is a report about what has already been done. Advice urges you to make something happen. News urges you to recognize something that has already happened and to respond to it. Advice says it is all up to you to act. News says someone else has acted."[6] Keller illustrates the difference between the two by highlighting the roles of military advisors and messengers in the ancient world. An enhanced version goes like this:

> Barbarians invade your country. Initial reports are devastating—death, destruction, and desolation. The king assembles his army to meet the foe, but his army is obliterated. The king's last heroic act is to send a wounded military advisor back to the capital city. What does this near-to-death military advisor do? He fearfully exhorts the inhabitants of the city to fight for their lives, "Archers on the wall! Cavalry at the west gate! Infantry on me!" The military advisor brings good advice about how to survive the impossible. The military advisor brings good advice on how to save yourself. The gospel or good news, however, is different. The king crushes the invading enemy, and then sends joyful messengers back to the fearful capital to announce the good news: "Victory! The king has won! Deliverance! Salvation!

---

6. Keller, *Hidden Christmas*, 21–22.

Life! Joy! Peace! Freedom! There is no more death! No more destruction! No more fear of doom! Stop fleeing! Stop trying to save yourselves!"[7]

The gospel is good news, which is the joyful message of the King's victory, of a victory won *for* us. Good advice is moralism, which is the desperate instruction to fight for your life, for a victory *still* needing to be achieved *by* us.

Good news is the announcement about something God has done, accomplished, or worked *for* us. Good advice is the instruction about something still needing to done, accomplished, or worked *by* us.

Therefore, good news is the report of God's victory for us in Christ. It says, "It is finished! Believe this!" Whereas good advice is instruction to attain an ever-elusive victory still in question. It says, "It is never finished! Be this! Do this!"

Preaching good news speaks people back to life again. God has done for us what we cannot do for ourselves. The Apostle Paul says the gospel is the power of God for a comprehensive victory or salvation (Rom 1:16). It is the power of God to justify, sanctify, and eventually glorify a messed-up people and creation. It reaches and renews lives, relationships, and places. It releases the personal active presence of Jesus Christ[8] and his achieved salvation into the world to justify, sanctify, and eventually glorify lives and the world.

This is why the Bible portrays the gospel as living and active words (Col 1:5–7) or as an "imperishable seed" that carries its own divine energies (1 Pet 1:23). The gospel seed is sown into human hearts carrying its own divine life and power. Therefore, it grows! The gospel does not need us, in fact, grows in spite of us. Therefore, the gospel establishes its own reality in the preaching event[9] or as it is heard (Rom 10:17). It does what it says. It creates a whole new world while being spoken. The gospel speaks us back to life again.

Preaching good advice (or the law) also does what it says or what God intends it to do. God intends the law to seal the Adamic-corpse in its coffin (Gal 3:16–22). "The Law of God has not made us better, but has instead shown us how sick we really are."[10] The law possesses a divine ministry of death, that is, of killing the Adamic-self wherever he or she is found so that Jesus and his salvation is one's only comfort in life and death. Therefore,

---

7. Keller, *Hidden Christmas*, 22.
8. Keller, *Prayer*, 54.
9. Bayer, *Martin Luther's Theology*, 251.
10. Large, *Mockingbird Devotional*, 244.

preaching good advice as a way to make us better and to improve our lives gets in the way of what God is primarily doing with his law in people's lives, both in the world and in the church (Gal 3–4).

Good advice cannot activate the Christian life. It enslaves instead, as it employs the law in an unlawful way that, frankly, is phenomenally addictive. We crave control. We are obsessed with being our own savior. Good advice becomes our heroin.

Theologically speaking, "good advice" is Pelagianism (or semi-Pelagianism if you add God's assisting hand to the mix). The inevitable and harmful result of good advice preaching is the spiritual formation of delusional Pharisees on the one hand, who by all appearances are spiritually crushing it, and depressed saints on the other, who did not drink the Kool-Aid and have convinced themselves they are on God's "B Team." Therefore, preaching good advice releases self-salvation into the world (Gal 3:1–3), whereas preaching good news releases Jesus Christ and his salvation into the world.

Lindbeck notes that it was the loss of good news as "the interpretive key to all of Scripture" after the Reformation that gave birth to many strange ways to read the Bible.[11] He argues for the recovery of Jesus Christ and his comprehensive salvation as "the interpretive key to all of Scripture."[12] This gospel lens should provide the basis for preaching and church unity, community, renewal, and witness in the world today, even while maintaining real differences and distinctions between the various bodies of church denominations and traditions.[13]

Therefore, preaching is about *good news* being believed, not *good advice* being followed. The Gospel Arc seeks to participate in good news preaching. Taking Jesus with you in preaching changes everything.

---

11. Lindbeck, *Church in a Postliberal Age*, 73.
12. Lindbeck, *Church in a Postliberal Age*, 72–3.
13. Lindbeck, *Church in a Postliberal Age*, 72–3.

PART 2

The Gospel Arc

Chapter 3

Introducing the Gospel Arc

The Gospel Arc takes Jesus with you in preaching. It is preaching that experiences Jesus with the Bible. Every Christian wants to experience Jesus. Well, let's pretend. Often the Bible is the last place we may look. Spiritual disciplines, church traditions, special anointed individuals[1], feeling Jesus immediately in our hearts, acts of the will, biblical principles, spiritual techniques, tapping into the mysterious movements of the Holy Spirit in this way and that, keeping the traditional law (think ten commandments) or the endless more progressive spiritual laws (the "quiet time," being a "fully devoted follower," going on a mission trip, social justice), and the medium of music are all ways we try to activate God's presence in our lives.

The Gospel Arc aims to experience Jesus with the Bible, thereby changing everything. In other words, the aim is to intentionally create space for the Holy Spirit to reach and renew the life of the preacher and listener with the biblical text during sermon preparation and proclamation.

The climax of the Gospel Arc is displaying an aspect of Jesus and his salvation in the biblical text in such a way that it is both clear to the mind and real to the heart. Thereby, a *Textual Jesus* is experienced by faith. In this way, both the preacher and listener are reached and renewed by Jesus with

---

1. Think of the exploding celebrity pastor phenomenon today via social media, podcasts, books, conferences, and other venues to access favorite pastors. The local pastor is now not enough in his eyes nor the eyes of his congregation. In other words, he competes with "pastor porn."

the Bible. "Those who preach with him in view, encounter him anew."[2] Taking Jesus with you in preaching changes everything.

THE BIBLE'S SIXTH SENSE

"I see dead people," says the young Cole Sear (Haley Joel Osment) to child psychologist Dr. Crowe (Bruce Willis) in M. Night Shyamalan's suspenseful thriller *The Sixth Sense* (1999). Cole's anxious confession during the movie's opening scenes is frighteningly meaningful, that is, truly creepy. And yet mysteriously, embedded in Cole's eerie words is a surplus of meaning to be discovered retrospectively at the movie's shocking ending.

Spoiler alert: Dr. Crowe is dead! This revelation changes everything. It is the final and full revelation of the movie and it is the movie's ultimate interpretive lens. Therefore, "Dr. Crowe is dead" opens up the whole movie, that is, we now see more. All previous meaningful content—including Cole's initial creepy confession, "I see dead people"—is now reinterpreted in the light of this ultimate revelation.

Therefore, "I see dead people" not only signified the original meaning in the movie's opening scenes, but it also carried a surplus of meaning to be discovered later (retrospectively) at the movie's end. "I see dead people" was true in its original meaning but just not exhaustive in its ultimate meaning. Once "Dr. Crowe is dead" blows up the movie, the surplus of meaning embedded in "I see dead people" is powerfully released upon the viewer— "What?! He's been dead the whole time!"

In this way, "I see dead people" is partial or incomplete in its meaning until "Dr. Crowe is dead" completes, fulfills, finalizes, escalates, or exhausts its meaning. Furthermore, it is important to note that the final revelation of "Dr. Crowe is dead" in no way contradicts or makes untrue the original previous meaning of "I see dead people"; it simply exhausts it.

From the perspective of the Gospel Arc preaching model, "I see dead people" is "Pole 1" in the revelatory arc of the movie. It is the original meaning of the movie's opening scenes. And "Dr. Crowe is dead" is "Pole 2" in the revelatory arc of the movie. It is the ultimate meaning of the unfolding storyline of the movie. Therefore, "I see dead people" (Pole 1) finds its final and full meaning in "Dr. Crowe is dead" (Pole 2). In this way, one reads forward in the language of the Gospel Arc.

Furthermore, in light of "Dr. Crowe is dead" (Pole 2), "I see dead people" (Pole 1) is revealed to carry a surplus of meaning inherently embedded

---

2. Dr. Todd Still came up with this phrase amidst our friendship and frequent discussions about preaching Jesus and his salvation in all the Bible.

within it but waiting to be discovered. In this way, one reads backwards in the language of the Gospel Arc. Therefore, meaning flows both ways between the "Poles."

The gospel is the Bible's "sixth sense." Jesus and his salvation is the final and full revelation of God. It is the ultimate storyline of the Bible and its exhaustive revelatory lens. The Gospel Arc seeks to employ the Bible's "Sixth Sense" in order to read, experience, and communicate the Bible.

Therefore, The Gospel Arc is not so much a fixed homiletical method as it is a way of seeing—a sixth sense. It recognizes the need for our Bible reading to be evangelized. It recognizes God as the real meaningful author of the Bible, not simply a "ghost writer" hidden behind the human authors. It utilizes an instinctive tapping into the way Jesus and the New Testament writers read the Bible.

In other words, the Gospel Arc sees the Bible as one ultimate, unfolding story of redemption climaxing in the incarnation, life, death, resurrection, and present reign of Jesus Christ. Jesus and his salvation *is* the final and full revelation of God, naturally opening up the Scriptures so that more is seen (Luke 24). Taking Jesus with you in preaching changes everything.

A TEXTUAL JESUS

Practically speaking, the Gospel Arc is preaching that builds around Jesus and his salvation in any given biblical text. It is preaching that builds around a *Textual Jesus*, that is, the Jesus in the text.

The Gospel Arc is an arc that connects two poles: Pole 1 and Pole 2. These two "Poles" are divinely connected, both historically and theologically. Pole 1 is the textual pole of a given passage in the Bible. Pole 2 is the contextual pole of the overall message of the Bible. Therefore, the Gospel Arc connects the original historical meaning of a biblical text (Pole 1) to the overall message of the Bible, the climax of God's revelation in Jesus Christ and his salvation (Pole 2).

The Gospel Arc starts with Pole 1 or the original historical meaning of the biblical text. Pole 1 is the message of the text or what the passage is *saying* and *doing* in its original historical context. The aim of the Gospel Arc in Pole 1 is to discover the original historical meaning of the biblical text by listening to the text (Round 1), understanding the text (Round 2), and discovering the message of the text (Round 3).

The Gospel Arc continues by connecting Pole 1 to Pole 2 or Jesus Christ and his salvation. Jesus Christ and his salvation (Pole 2) is not only the ultimate message of the whole Bible but also of the specific biblical text being considered (Pole 1). Pole 2 is the climax of God's revelation, the ultimate revelatory lens for reading the Bible. Pole 2 is the redemptive-historical meaning of the original historical text. Pole 2 is the ultimate message of a specific text to reach and renew lives, the home, relationships, the church, communities, and the surrounding culture.

Pole 2 changes everything, including how to read the Bible. Pole 2 retrospectively rereads, re-narrates, or reinterprets all previous revelation (Pole 1). Pole 2 involves, fulfills, escalates, corresponds to, completes, addresses, satisfies, perfects, resolves, or maps more meaning onto all previous revelation (Pole 1). Therefore, a biblical text has not been properly understood, applied, or communicated until its original message (Pole 1) has been integrated with the overall message of the Bible culminating in Jesus Christ and his salvation (Pole 2).

There are two ways to connect or integrate the biblical text (Pole 1) to Jesus Christ and his salvation (Pole 2), and the meaning flows both ways:

1. Read forward from the text to Jesus Christ and his salvation.
2. Read backwards from Jesus Christ and his salvation to the text.

The aim of connecting or integrating Pole 1 to Pole 2 is to form a specific Gospel Arc or *Textual Jesus* from the text to build a sermon around that reaches and renews lives, the home, relationships, the church, communities, and the surrounding culture.

In sum, the aim of the Gospel Arc preaching model is a *Textual Jesus* to be experienced by faith to reach and renew the world (Rom 1:16). The Gospel Arc preaching model involves five "Rounds" of work: 1) Rounds 1–3 involve discovering Pole 1, 2) Round 4 seeks to connect or integrate Pole 1 to Pole 2 to form a textually specific Jesus or *Textual Jesus*, and 3) Round 5 seeks to build a sermon around the *Textual Jesus* that is clear to the mind and real to the heart. Therefore, the Gospel Arc is an attempt to take Jesus with you in preaching.

TAKE JESUS WITH YOU IN PREACHING

Any preaching model that seeks to create space for the Holy Spirit to work gospel renewal with the Bible into the life and ministry of the preacher and hearer has the potential to transform lives, the home, relationships, the church, communities, the culture, and the world. Any preaching model that seeks to redress preaching's moralistic tendency is of great value for the church and the world. Any preaching model that seeks to align itself with the apostolic practice and power of nothing but "Christ crucified" participates with the power of God for a comprehensive salvation (1 Corinthians 2:2).

Therefore, an intentional preaching model that seeks to experience Jesus and his salvation with the Bible by faith has the potential to produce a gospel movement in a specific place by the work of the Holy Spirit. The Gospel Arc preaching model seeks this kind of impact.

Those unfamiliar with Christocentric preaching may benefit from the Gospel Arc's accessible approach. It is a way of seeing and communicating the Bible—a sixth sense. It is a lens through which to understand more than a list of steps to follow.

Those familiar with Christocentric preaching may benefit from the Gospel Arc's intentional textual approach. It is a way to discover, experience, and deliver a specific aspect of Jesus Christ and his salvation from the text to reach and renew lives. In this way, the Gospel Arc avoids a jumping-over-the-text-to-Jesus approach that some Christocentric preaching practices. Thereby, it avoids boring hearers with a shallow and strangely repetitive Jesus floating above the text and peoples' lives. The Gospel Arc seeks a biblically *Textual Jesus*.

If the Gospel Arc preaching model is effective and worthwhile, then it should be a culturally adaptable model. It targets the universal human need to experience Jesus Christ and his salvation with the Bible more than the instruction and exhortation of inevitable culturally-bound "biblical applications." All people and cultures are in need of good news, not good advice, and the Gospel Arc seeks to deliver good news to universal human conditions, needs, or burdens.

Finally, preachers can and should seek to experience continual gospel renewal in their lives and ministries by employing a multiform approach to the means of grace.[3] The Gospel Arc, however, is specifically designed to create space for the preacher to experience gospel renewal during sermon preparation and proclamation—in other words, during the work of their primary call. Therefore, those who preach with him in view, encounter him anew. Taking Jesus with you in preaching changes everything.

---

3. A means of grace is the "outward means whereby Christ communicates to us the benefits of his mediation" (*Westminster Standards*, Westminster Larger Catechism Question, 154, 62). Historically, the means of grace have been the Scriptures, the sacraments, the preached Word, prayer, public worship, and Christian friendship at work in worship, community, nurture, service, the making of new friends and having gospel conversations, ministry, and other manifestations of the inseparable realities of church and mission.

THE PRACTICE AND POWER OF THE GOSPEL ARC

How to Use this Book

Resources for preaching tend to walk the tightrope between practice and principle or instruction and biblical-theological power. The tension is real. Perhaps it is better to simply explore one or the other rather than attempt both, but regardless, The Gospel Arc stubbornly attempts both. It leads with the practical because most biblical communicators crave the concrete. Simultaneously, it connects the concrete to its present biblical-theological power. Therefore, with this dual approach, the aim is to not only shape the message but also the messenger.

The Gospel Arc preaching model involves five rounds of practical sermon work for any given Biblical text. This book will lay out each round in order, providing its: 1) description, 2) instruction, 3) example, and 4) biblical-theological power. With this plan, the aim is to communicate practice and principle simultaneously to maximize effectiveness.

For immediate use and rapid reference at any time, the complete Gospel Arc Preaching Manual is provided next (and also in Appendix I). It is designed to walk you through any biblical text to help discover and communicate the *Textual Jesus* present in the text, awaiting experience by faith.

Perhaps the Gospel Arc Preaching Manual is sufficient for your needs and no further reading is needed. Just in case, however, the rest of the book unpacks each round of the Gospel Arc Preaching Manual (five rounds total) with more comprehensive coverage. Next, the biblical-theological power for the Gospel Arc (its energies) are presented for each round to provoke thought and promote space for gospel renewal.

In sum, this book can be read at both practical and biblical-theological levels. Practically, you can immediately implement the five rounds of the Gospel Arc preaching model. Biblically-theologically, you can explore the present power that informs, forms, and energizes each individual round.

Chapter 4

The Gospel Arc Preaching Manual

Round 1: Listen to the Text

Pole 1
*The Original Historical Meaning

Pole 2
*The Ultimate Overall Meaning of all Scripture
(Jesus Christ and His Salvation)

The Gospel Arc

LISTEN TO THE TEXT

1. Listen for Yourself (become an "intelligent mystic"):

2. Listen to the World of the Text (enter into the life of the text—its sights, sounds, and scents . . . the world of the text must come before our ideas about it . . . the world of the text must be allowed to shape our ideas rather than vice-versa):

3. Listen for Others (become a "physician of the soul"):

Listening Tool:

- Listen to God in and with the text
- Luxuriate in the text
- Slow, gentle reading
- A spontaneous, even naïve engagement with the text
- Learning to listen, think, feel, see, imagine, encounter, and ask questions of the text in the presence of God
- Imagination and empathy come first, and analysis comes second
- The Bible is a "stranger thing", admit it and be curious

An Example from Rom. 10:1–4.

Each chapter in Part 3, Doing the Gospel Arc, includes an example from this passage for each of the five rounds.

Round 2: Understand the Text

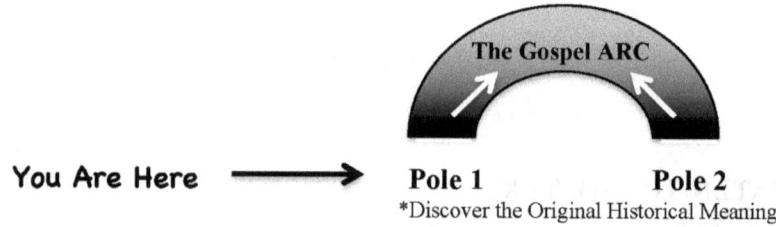

The Gospel Arc

UNDERSTAND THE TEXT

1. Create a Textual Map (itemize main and supporting ideas):
2. Write a Running Commentary (answer significant questions in the text—literary, historical, theological . . . employ study aids after some sweat equity in the text):

Interpretive Tool (pay special attention to significant):

- Words
- Ideas
- Images
- Repetitions
- Connector words
- Allusions and quotes from other places in the Bible
- Characters and dialogue
- Scenes and places
- Actions and events
- Historical background
- The unexpected, unusual surprises, out of place details, and questions that provoke you in the text (great place for the deepest meaning to hide)

An Example from Rom. 10:1–4.

Each chapter in Part 3, Doing the Gospel Arc, includes an example from this passage for each of the five rounds.

Round 3: Discover the Text's Message

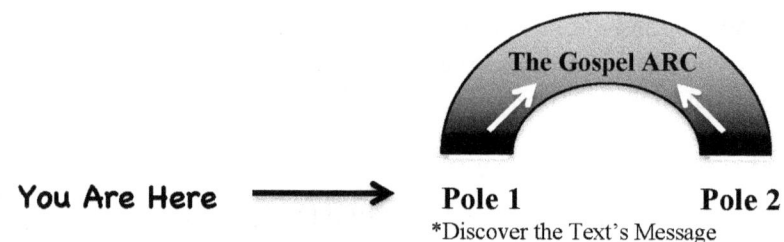

The Gospel Arc

DISCOVER THE TEXT'S MESSAGE

1. Identify a particular aspect of the *Human Condition* (HC) addressed in the text.

Human Condition Tool (record in a sticky statement or vivid image):

- What is the *God-sized* or *God-shaped* "hole" found in the text due to the functional impact of the absence of God upon the human condition (i.e., the fallen condition is both deprived and depraved)?
- What is the *"mental map"* (way of seeing) and/or *"heart map"* (way of trusting) of the individual people and/or corporate people (culture) in the text?
- What is the universal human need, burden, condition, or conflict in or behind the text?
- Who are the *people* or what are the *places* in view in the text?
- What is the universal human condition of the participants and/or hearers being addressed?
- What required the writing of this text?
- Why might the Holy Spirit have inspired the text?
- What is the universal human need, burden, condition, or conflict in the text that requires the grace of Jesus Christ and his salvation?

- What are the *background beliefs* or *alternate beliefs* in the text that correspond to your hearers in order to *connect* (point of contact) and *challenge* (push on pressure point) and ultimately *re-connect* (re-enchant with the gospel)?
- What is the *idol*, god-replacement, substitute-savior, or self-salvation strategy in the text?

2. Identify the Primary Thing the Text is *Saying* or the *Big Idea* of the Text.

Big Idea Tool (record in a sticky statement or vivid image):

- What is the primary powerful thing the text is *saying*?
- What is the dominant thought, idea, image, story, need, "Aha!," subject, theme, or content in the text?
- What is the "freshly squeezed" essence of the text?
- This text is about _____.
- The "Speech" in Speech-Act.

3. Identify the primary thing the text is *doing* with what it is saying or the *Applied Big Idea* of the text. Because God's Word *does* what it *says*!

Applied Big Idea Tool (record in a sticky statement or vivid image):

- What is the primary powerful thing the text is *doing* with what it is saying?
- Where is the passage *going*?
- Where is the passage *taking us*?
- What is the *"so what?,"* force, function, movement, intention, action, practical difference, or transformative possibility of the controlling content?
- This text is doing _____.
- What are the energies being imparted by the text?
- The "Act" in Speech-Act.
- How the gospel re-enchants lives, relationships, communities, places, all of life (the world).

Literary Tool:

- If the text is *narrative literature* or a *story*, then discover how the setting, characters, conflict or plot line, and resolution or lack thereof communicate the three interpretive textual tracks (i.e., the human condition, the Big Idea, and the Applied Big Idea of the text).
- If the text is *propositional literature* or a *logical argument*, then discover how the flow of the main and supporting ideas communicate the three interpretive textual tracks.
- If the text is *law* or an *ethical principle*, then discover how the ideal or anti-ideal communicate the three interpretive textual tracks.
- If the text is *wisdom literature*, then discover how the *fabric of creation* (i.e., the regular patterns or order in creation) or the *futility of creation* (i.e., the irregular patterns or active de-creation because of sin in creation) communicates the three interpretive textual tracks.
- If the text is *poetic literature*, then discover how the image that brings the *world of ideas* and the the *world of experience* together communicates the three interpretive textual tracks.
- If the text is *apocalyptic literature*, then discover how the visual revelation (rather than aural) communicates the three interpretive textual tracks.

An Example from Rom. 10:1–4.

Each chapter in Part 3, Doing the Gospel Arc, includes an example from this passage for each of the five rounds.

Round 4: Discover the Textual Jesus

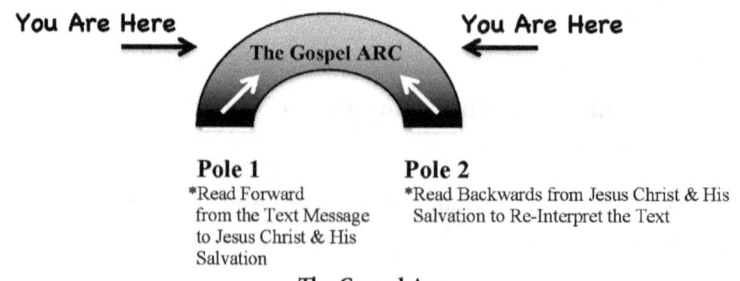

The Gospel Arc

DISCOVER THE TEXTUAL JESUS

1. *Read forward* by following the divinely embedded *Gospel Threads* in the text. These threads carry a *surplus of meaning* (think it out below).

Gospel Thread Tool (Pole 1 gives a *pattern of significance* to Jesus Christ and his salvation):

- An *attribute* and/or *action of God* in the text that is addressing the universal human condition, need, or burden in the text. Follow this gospel thread to its ultimate example or embodiment in Jesus Christ and his salvation.
- A *theme* or *idea* in the text. Follow this gospel thread to its ultimate resolution in Jesus Christ and his salvation.
- A *law* or *biblical ethic* in the text. Follow this gospel thread to its completion in Jesus Christ and his salvation.
- An *image* in the text. Follow this gospel thread to its ultimate target in Jesus Christ and his salvation.
- A *type* or *pattern* in the text. Follow this gospel thread to its ultimate fulfillment, substance, or perfection in Jesus Christ and his salvation.
- A *story of an individual or community* in the text. Follow this gospel thread to its ultimate bigger story of Jesus Christ and his salvation.
- An *instinct* or *sense* in the text. Follow this gospel thread to its ultimate convergence on Jesus Christ and his salvation.
- A *sin and its consequences*, a *heart and life issue*, a *cultural heart and life issue*, a *spiritual need*, a *universal human "hole," condition, burden, and problem* in the text. Follow these gospel threads to their ultimate solution in Jesus Christ and his salvation.
- The *human longing in the text*. Follow this gospel thread to its ultimate satisfaction in JesusChrist and his salvation.
- The *functional human trust*, hope, love, worship, salvation, justification, or God-replacement in the text. Follow this gospel thread to its ultimate source and satisfaction in Jesus Christ and his salvation.
- The *grace at work in the text*. Follow this gospel thread to its ultimate source in Jesus Christ and his salvation.

2. *Read backwards* by looking through the *Gospel Lens* to re-interpret or find the *surplus of meaning in the text* (think it out below).

Gospel Lens Tool (Pole 2 *maps more meaning* onto, completes, or reinterprets Pole 1):

Look at how Jesus and his salvation:

- Address the universal human need, condition, or burden in the text.
- Address what the text is *saying* (i.e., the ultimate Big Idea of the text).
- Accomplish what the text is *doing* (i.e., the ultimate Applied Big Idea of the text).
- Solve tensions in the text.
- Involve, correspond to, map more meaning onto, fulfill, escalate, or complete the signifiers (gospel threads) in the text.
- Interpret the Old Testament allusions, echoes, or quotations in the New Testament text.
- Provide the source or ultimate work of grace in the text.

3. Craft the specific *Textual Jesus* in the text into *one* sticky statement or vivid image (this freshly crafted *Textual Jesus* is what the sermon is built around):

Textual Jesus Tool:

- Connect Pole 1 and Pole 2 to each other to form a Gospel Arc. This is your *Textual Jesus*.
- Take 2 lumps of clay (Pole 1 and Pole 2) and craft ONE specific aspect of Jesus Christ and his salvation from the text.
- What is a specific aspect of Jesus Christ and his salvation in the text to reach and renew lives, relationships, places, the world?
- Locate the Jesus of the text or the Word in the Word.

An Example from Rom. 10:1–4.

Each chapter in Part 3, Doing the Gospel Arc, includes an example from this passage for each of the five rounds.

Round 5: Craft a Sermon Message

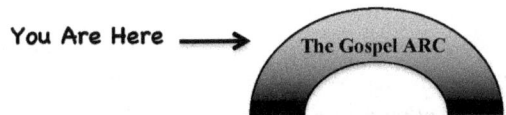

*Build the Sermon Around the *Textual Jesus*
**A Gospel ARC Sermon is Built Around Re-Presenting Jesus Christ & His Salvation according to the Particular Way of the Text in a Way that is Clear to the Mind and Real to the Heart

The Gospel Arc

CRAFT A SERMON MESSAGE

1. The sermon should say and do *one powerful thing* not many things. Therefore, craft a *Sermon Message*. Pick a point!

Sermon Message Tool 1:

First, a sermon message is crafted around the five interpretive tracks below:

1. Your recorded sticky statement or vivid image for the *universal human and/or cultural condition* being specifically addressed in the text.
2. Your recorded sticky statement or vivid image for the text's *Big Idea* (or the primary thing the passage is saying).
3. Your recorded sticky statement or vivid image for the text's *Applied Big Idea* (or the primary thing the passage is doing with what it is saying).
4. Your recorded sticky statement or vivid image for the *Textual Jesus* (or the specific aspect of Jesus Christ and his salvation revealed in the text).
5. The specific human and/or cultural need of *contemporary hearers* (the local listening need).

Sermon Message Tool 2:

Second, there are three preferred ways to craft a Sermon Message around the five interpretive tracks above:

1. *Blend them all together* into one *sticky statement, vivid image,* or *suspenseful question*. Whether blended together into one sticky statement, vivid image, or suspenseful question, the individual tracks become the supporting ideas or movements of the Sermon Map.

    Sticky Statement:
    Vivid Image:
    or Suspenseful Question:

2. *Lead with one track while the other tracks stand off stage* waiting to make key appearances during the event of the sermon. In other words, the lead track rules them all by becoming the Sermon Message and the other tracks play key supporting roles as needed in the Sermon Map.

    Lead Track:
    Supporting Track(s):

3. *Follow a narrative form* that places the individual tracks into the plot line of one ultimate over-arching story or Sermon Message. In other words, "This is a story about ___." What you fill in is your Sermon Message. How you tell the story is your Sermon Map.

    This is a story about _____." This is your Sermon Message:
    Tell the story with the individual Interpretive Tracks (Sermon Map):

2. Once you have *Crafted a Sermon Message,* build everything around it. *Build A Sermon Map* in oral form (natural scripting to be heard not read). Keep in mind:

- The aim of preaching is to experience Jesus Christ and his salvation with the text in order to reach and renew lives, the home, relationships, the church, places, communities, and the surrounding culture.
- In other words, the aim of preaching is gospel-growth in people.
- Therefore, the Sermon Map should best support this aim.

An Example from Rom. 10:1–4.

Each chapter in Part 3, Doing the Gospel Arc, includes an example from this passage for each of the five rounds.

PART 3

Doing the Gospel Arc

Chapter 5

Listen to the Text

Preaching that experiences Jesus with the Bible begins with "Round 1: Listen to the Text." As the preacher approaches the text, he should come with the prayerful expectation of listening to God in and with the text. By listening to the text, we can expect to be personally reached and renewed by God in and with the text. In other words, we are coming to the text ready to experience Jesus and his salvation by faith. As we read the Scriptures, we pray that our mental and emotional faculties are ignited by the Jesus we find in the Scriptures. This is "intelligent mysticism."[1] Listening to God in the text, we find Jesus waiting in the text for us, coming to give us himself: the gospel.

Pole 1
*The Original Historical Meaning

Pole 2
*The Ultimate Overall Meaning of all Scripture (Jesus Christ and His Salvation)

The Gospel Arc

---

1. See Luke 24. "Intelligent mystic" comes from Murray, *Redemption: Accomplished and Applied*, 169.

Round 1: Listen to the Text

1. Listen for Yourself (become an "intelligent mystic"):
2. Listen to the World of the Text (enter into the life of the text—its sights, sounds, and scents . . . the world of the text must come before our ideas about it . . . the world of the text must be allowed to shape our ideas rather than vice-versa):
3. Listen for Others (become a "physician of the soul"):

Listening Tool:

- Listen to God in and with the text
- Luxuriate in the text
- Slow, gentle reading
- A spontaneous, even naïve engagement with the text
- Learning to listen, think, feel, see, imagine, encounter, and ask questions of the text in the presence of God
- Imagination and empathy come first, and analysis comes second
- The Bible is a "stranger thing", admit it and be curious

INSTRUCTION

"Shut up and listen!" All good Bible reading begins this way.

Listening to the text begins with the divine energies of the Word. It begins with "stranger things," that is, a personal active presence in the Bible.[2] Listening to the text comes to the Bible with empty hands that need to be filled. It creates space for the Holy Spirit to connect the living and active Word(s) of the text to the communicator during the initial movements of sermon preparation. A fresh encounter with Jesus and his salvation by faith each time we read the text will often cause us to approach the text with an excited, expectant, and even naive engagement with the text, regardless of our level of textual familiarity.

Listening to the text is a slow, gentle reading of the text. No rushing through the textual terrain. It is a relaxing read, absent of the need to control

---

2. Keller, *Prayer: Experiencing Awe and Intimacy with God*, 54.

and master the text. Listening to the text means God is at work in, with, and through the reading of the text to speak us back to life again. God sets the agenda, not us. The Bible imparts its divine energies.

Since the Bible imparts its own energies, there is freedom to experience what strikes us in the text, what is impressed upon us by the text, the strangeness of the text, a hidden "aha" embedded in the text, the blunt force of the text, and our own need and weakness exposed by the text. The aim of listening to the text is learning to listen to God in and with the text. In other words, to experience Jesus with the Bible.

Generally speaking, listening to the text leads to meditation or thinking in the presence of God, which naturally turns into prayer and communion with God. As God speaks, there is something to think about and talk about with Him. In this way, listening to the text creates space for the Holy Spirit to work gospel renewal or gospel growth into the life and ministry of the preacher with the text during the initial moments of sermon preparation.

Practically, listening to the text means reading the text at least three times. Each reading is a time to luxuriate in the text, a time to engage the text in a slow, gentle reading with fresh eyes and an expectant ear. Fred Craddock encourages a "spontaneous, even naive engagement with the text."[3]

Record keeping for each reading of the text should be significant thoughts in simple form. The goal is not the posthumous discovery of your sermon notes for publication, but a simple record of your meaningful interaction with God in the text. What is impressed upon you and strikes you is more likely to be personally significant, sermonically significant, and helpful for others.

Listen for Yourself

The first reading is listening for yourself. This is a time to soak your soul in the text. In other words, become an "intelligent mystic"[4] who connects with God with the text, not apart from it.

It would not be uncommon for the preacher, having been recently emptied the previous Sunday filling others up, to expectantly be put back together again during this first reading. Listening for yourself is life-giving. It is your primal need connecting with God and His good words. It is learning to read, think on (meditate), pray, and experience the wonder of the Word for yourself.

---

3. Craddock, *Preaching*, 105.
4. Murray, *Redemption: Accomplished and Applied*, 169.

This first reading has no agenda but to listen and receive from God in and with His Word. The Bible imparts its own energies to us. Therefore, rest is a big deal in this first reading, the exact opposite of striving to make something happen. The spiritual and emotional payoff is learning to relax, rely, and rejoice in God with His Word. Not only are personal burdens frequently and noticeably unloaded on the Burden-Bearer at this time, but also the more subconscious burden of "producing" a sermon each week. Cease striving, be still, and know God is your Lord and Savior in this first reading.

Listen to the World of the Text

The second reading is listening to the world of the text. This obviously does not exclude listening to God with the text for yourself. It simply means God loves the world, too. This is a time to enter the life of the text . . . to connect with the flesh, bones, and blood of the text . . . to engage the sights, sounds, and scents of the text. In other words, intentionally avoid a long-distance relationship with the text.

Therefore, make the text *real* by entering its world. Immerse yourself in the world of the text. Engage its senses . . . feel its forces . . . drink its drama. Play Sherlock Holmes and be incredibly curious about the text. Look at the person(s) speaking in the text. Carefully observe the actions and events in the text. Feel the emotional temperature of the text. Walk around the background and surroundings of the text. Relate to the relationships in the text.

For example, listen to "Let there be light!" and watch God's Word do what it says. Sing Adam's love song, that is, the first recorded words of a human being. Watch the weird mingling of heavenly and earthly creatures at the intersection of the garden. Is this why Adam and Eve don't freak out at the sight of the snake? Taste the forbidden fruit. Feel the world change as sin, death, and evil invade and enslave.

In other words, touch ideas, imagine images, interview characters, see scenes, replay actions, feel feelings, and question the unexpected. Learn to think and feel in the presence of God as the biblical text inflames your imagination. As far as the text goes, so goes your imagination.

Listening to the world of the text is learning to listen, think, feel, see, imagine, encounter, experience, connect to, and ask questions of the text in the presence of God. It is letting the world of the text inform and ignite your ideas rather than the other way around. It would not be uncommon for the preacher to ask God why a passage seems strange, asking questions of the world of the text in the presence of God.

Listen for Others

The third reading is listening for others. This is a time to love others with the text by considering them in light of the text. It is learning to love others while being loved back to life again by God with the text. In other words, become a physician of the soul who listens on behalf of the multiform needs, conditions, and burdens of others. For example, how would a divorced single parent, irreligious person, or someone struggling with same sex desires hear this text?

Therefore, anticipate the other's *initial* response, expectation, interpretation, thinking, feeling, questions, objections, or overall human condition before this text. Do not do an in depth "background check." Simply pay attention to your immediate first impressions of another hearing the text. Exercise rapid reflection, not in-depth analysis.

Pay attention, obviously, to those with whom you do life, ministry, or lead; those to whom you minister (both inside and outside the church), counsel, or engage in some form of pastoral care, and generally those with whom you are friends, acquaintances, or have gospel conversations. Since the mission of the local church is to reach and renew as many people as possible with the gospel in its community, consider those yet to be reached (the unchurched) as well as those needing to be renewed (the over-churched) by the gospel in your community.

Pay attention to *fluid beliefs* and narratives around you, especially the current "big thing." Yes, they are short-lived; yes, they recycle into a new form every couple years. They are a big deal, however, to many listening to your text and are an easy open door for the gospel (Col 4:3–4). Also, routinely give attention to more *fixed beliefs of unbelief* around you. They stick around for a reason.[5]

Last, some of the engaging listeners of the text are real and fictional characters in books, articles, movies, entertainment, music, sports, social media, print media, big media companies, and so on, and in your own imagination. Pick a character or two who intrigue you. Perhaps it is something they think, feel, experience, say, or do that strikes you. Then consider, "How would they hear this text?" If there are no interesting people in your world, make some up! For example, picture a twenty-something dude named Bob. He grew up in the church, knows his Bible, was active in youth ministry, and was active in campus ministry, which is where he met Sue. Two weeks before their wedding she calls it off—Sue is in love with someone else. How does Bob hear this text?

---

5. I have found Timothy Keller's *The Reason For God* and *Making Sense of God* helpful resources for interacting with the more fixed alternative beliefs to Christianity today.

AN EXAMPLE FROM ROMANS 10:1-4

Listen for Yourself:

- Paul's heart is shaped by substitution. Mine feels full of me.
- How can there be intense passion for God and dedication to God without a true knowledge of God? What does this look like in a person's life, relationships, the home, or the church?
- Paul seems to be making a stunning claim: a true knowledge of God begins, grows, and develops by grasping the righteousness from God.
- "Oh God, may the righteousness *from you* become more and more clear to my mind and real to my heart."

Listen to the World of the Text:

- Is Paul claiming x-ray vision into the human heart, that is, its motivational roots, in v.2? I've accused my accusers countless times saying, "Are you assuming my motives?" Paul seems to be saying, "Yes, I am, as a God appointed witness."
- The world of this text feels like a deep struggle. A struggle far deeper than a pandemic, riots, racial unrest, a culture war, bad doctrine, and political power plays. Is the struggle of v.3 the deepest struggle in the cosmos, the human heart, relationships, the home, the church, communities, racial strife, power struggles, culture wars, and more?
- Why does Paul say, "they did not *submit* to the righteousness from God"? Why doesn't he say, "they did not *receive* the righteousness from God"? Submission feels impersonal, cold, and forced. It sounds like something a control freak and self-important person would say, "Submit, damnit!" It conjures up images of slaves and other unhappy people. Or am I missing something (ignorant) about the idea of "submission"? Isn't there a more energizing, attractive, joyful, freeing, or happier way to relate to the righteousness from God?

Listen for Others:

- How do people in a pandemic hear this text?
- How do peaceful protesters, violent rioters, political powers, culture warriors, Marxist anarchists, the "woke," and the church hear this text?
- How does selective outrage hear this text?
- How does anxiety and depression hear this text?
- There feels like a lot of "zeal without knowledge" going on today.

Chapter 6

Understand the Text

Listening to the text comes first; analysis comes second. The aim in "Round 2: Understand the Text," is to continue the process started in "Round 1: Listen to the Text," that is, to discover *Pole 1* of the *Gospel Arc* or the original historical meaning of the text.

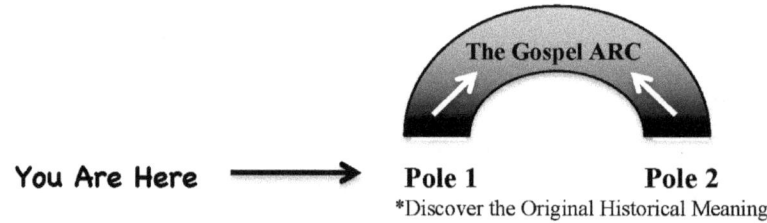

The Gospel Arc

ROUND 2: UNDERSTAND THE TEXT

1. Create a *Textual Map* (itemize main and supporting ideas):

2. Write a *Running Commentary* (answer significant questions in the text—literary, historical, theological . . . employ study aids after some sweat equity in the text):

Interpretive Tool (pay special attention to significant):

- Words
- Ideas
- Images
- Repetitions
- Connector words
- Allusions and quotes from other places in the Bible
- Characters and dialogue
- Scenes and places
- Actions and events
- Historical background
- The unexpected, unusual surprises, out of place details, and questions that provoke you in the text (great place for the deepest meaning to hide)

INSTRUCTION

The mechanics involved in the work of freshly squeezing meaning from the text vary and are not in short supply. The Gospel Arc employs two primary tools to understand the text: 1) a *Textual Map* with a 2) *Running Commentary*.[1] Every text is a forest of living and active words or meaning. The *Textual Map* navigates the forest of the text by mapping it. The *Running Commentary* engages and enjoys the individual trees of the text by analyzing them.

---

1. "Running Commentary" has been cannibalized from Keller, *Preaching: Communicating Faith in an Age of Skepticism*, 216.

Create a Textual Map

Every text has a textual terrain consisting of main and supporting ideas. The aim of the *Textual Map* is to map them, that is, to itemize them. Therefore, map the text by itemizing its main and supporting ideas.

Practically, start with the literary form of the text:

1. If the text is *narrative literature* or a *story*, then discover how the setting, characters, conflict or plot line, and resolution or lack thereof communicate main and supporting ideas.

2. If the text is *propositional literature* or a *logical argument*, then discover how the flow of ideas and images communicates main and supporting ideas.

3. If the text is *law* or an *ethical principle*, then discover how the ideal or anti-ideal communicates main and supporting ideas.

4. If the text is *wisdom literature*, then discover how the *fabric of creation* (i.e., the regular patterns or order in creation) or the *futility of creation* (i.e., the irregular patterns or active de-creation because of sin in creation) communicates main and supporting ideas.

5. If the text is *poetic literature*, then discover how the images that brings the *world of ideas* and the *world of experience* together communicate main and supporting ideas.

6. If the text is *apocalyptic literature*, then discover how the visual revelation (rather than aural) communicates main and supporting ideas.

Take, for example, Luke 7:1–10. Main idea number one might be from the *sick servant* (character): the need for healing (v. 2). A supporting idea might come from the *leaders of the Jews* (characters): healing by works or by being worthy (vv. 3–5). Another supporting idea might come from the warrior centurion (character): healing by faith or by not being worthy (vv. 6–7a). A final supporting idea might come from Jesus (character): healing by grace (v. 6a). Main idea number two might come from Jesus (character): faith deeply moves Jesus (v. 9). A supporting idea might come from the warrior centurion (character): because faith trusts in the healing power of Jesus' words (vv. 7b–8). Another supporting idea might come from the *setting*: because healing comes by the power of Jesus' words (6:19; 7:1). Last, main idea number 3 might come from the healing of the servant (action): faith alone heals (Luke 7.10).

Even if you fly blind without the literary form of the text, its main and supporting ideas can be intuitively discovered by asking:

1. What are the *main ideas* being communicated in the text?
2. What are the *supporting ideas* of the main ideas being communicated in the text?

A helpful *Textual Map* identifies at least two main ideas from the text. If you only identify one main idea, keep working. If, however, you still only come up with the same one main idea, then you might have discovered the *Big Idea* of the text, that is, the primary thing the text is *saying*. Great job! Now, work backwards from the *Big Idea* to discover some things being said about it. Ask what the text is saying about the *Big Idea*. The answers are the main ideas for your *Textual Map*.

Next, unpack those main ideas by discovering their respective supporting ideas from the text. Once completed, you now have a *Textual Map* of itemized main and supporting ideas. Now, you are cutting with the grain of the text. You are working with the meaning and energies of the text, rather than against them.

Your *Textual Map* can be as concrete as an outline that simply records main ideas and their supporting ideas. Or it can be as creative as a diagram, visually laying out the storyline of the text. There is freedom to learn and develop a personalized way to map out the main and supporting ideas of the text. If needed, break free from any training that shackles you to a specific "right way." If helpful, cannibalize a variety of approaches to create your own *Frankenstein Textual Map* that is personally energizing to work with.[2]

The significance of your *Textual Map* lies in its visual powers. It helps you "see" the textual terrain, enhancing your observation, understanding, and internalization of the text. In this way, the original historical message of the text becomes clearer to the mind and more real to the heart as the Holy Spirit works in, with, and during your work in the text.

Write a Running Commentary

The aim of the *Running Commentary* is to analyze the text. It is to freshly squeeze meaning from the text. Analyzing the text fills in, fills up, and fills out the *Textual Map* with lively active meaning. If the *Textual Map* is the

---

2. Be an exegetical and homiletical mad scientist and construct your own Frankenstein Textual Map. The following have been helpful to me: Chapell, *Christ-Centered Preaching*, Greidanus, *Modern Preacher and the Ancient Text*, Greidanus, *Preaching Christ from the Old Testament*, Goldsworthy, *Preaching the Whole Bible as Christian Scripture*, Keller, *Preaching: Communicating Faith in an Age of Skepticism*, Lloyd-Jones, *Preaching & Preachers*, Logan, *Preacher and Preaching*, Leithart, *Deep Exegesis*, Robinson, *Biblical Preaching*.

skeletal structure of the text then the *Running Commentary* is its internal organs. Both together, comprise the living and active body of the text.

The key to analyzing the text is learning to be selective, not all trees in the forest are significant. The *Running Commentary* answers the significant literary, historical, and theological questions in the text. For example, it will give special attention to notable:

- Words
- Ideas
- Images
- Repetitions
- Connector words
- Allusions and quotes from other places in the Bible
- Characters and dialogue
- Scenes and places
- Actions and events
- Historical background
- The unexpected, unusual surprises, out of place details, and questions that provoke you in the text (great place for the deepest meaning to hide)

Obviously, some of the above can overlap each other in a given text. For example, a *key word* can also be a *repetition*. Think of a *key word* as something like "propitiation." If you come across "propitiation" in the text, you need to know what *that* words means!

Key ideas and *images* are usually identified because their presence dominates the text. You cannot get around them; they stand in your way; they must be dealt with. In other words, you must interpret them. One way to interpret significant ideas in the text is to restate them in your own words. Often, restating forces interpretation. One way to interpret significant images in the text is to do a quick three-step dance: 1) identify the image, "shepherd," 2) identify the target of the image, "Lord," 3) interpret what the image is saying about its target, "the Lord is personally and actively present with his people."

What about *characters* and *dialogue* in the text? First, remember the Bible is not like James Ussher's classic, *The Annals of the World*, that is, an exhaustive history of the world. Rather, it is a highly selective theological history. Historical characters and dialogue matter greatly. The history is selective; the interpretation is theological.

For example, the Israelites (characters) watch in horror as Pharaoh and his army (more characters) rapidly approach with shock and awe. The Israelites speak forth their desperation (dialogue), rightly interpreting their doom and utter inability to save themselves. When God (the unexpected character) miraculously delivers by way of splitting the sea, Pharaoh (the self-reliant and therefore blind character) dramatically interprets the event wrongly. Pharaoh fails to bring his interpretive "A-game" because he only sees himself.

Actions and *events* in the Bible (just like characters and dialogue) can be historical or non-historical. In other words, historical characters tell stories all the time in the Bible. For example, the prophet Nathan tells his "poor little lamb story" to David in order to reveal David to David, "You are the man!" (2 Sam 12:7). Jesus, also, tells many parables that "have done more to upset his students' understanding than to give it a helping hand."[3]

Actions and events not only have the potential to reveal universal human conditions in the text, but also specific aspects of God and his grace that address those human conditions. For example, Moses and David profusely perform redemptive actions in the Bible that are designed to reveal God, not them. A classic is David and Goliath. "Be like David and kill the faith-killers (Goliaths) in your life!" I wore this approach out in campus ministry to inspire and motivate evangelism. Why, however, is it that we usually identify ourselves with David? Why not Goliath? Or the Philistines? Exactly . . . the primary reading of those texts is not, "Be like them," but rather, "Jesus is like them, only better."

The unexpected, unusual, surprises, out of place details, and questions that provoke one in the text are all great places for the deepest meaning to hide. Nine times out of ten they hide the *Textual Jesus*. That is, they provide a gospel thread in the text that leads to Jesus. So, follow the thread. These gospel threads provide a pattern of significance that are divinely designed to point to specific aspects of Jesus and his salvation. Think of the Marvel Comic artist who first drew the stick figure that became the Superhero, like Thor or Captain America. The artistic process is correspondingly progressive, not a Darwinian jump in species. In this way, most unsolved mysteries, unanswerable questions, and incomplete stories in the Old Testament are solved, answered, and completed by the final revelation of Jesus and his salvation.

For example, who isn't disturbed by God's command to Abraham to sacrifice his own son, Isaac? If you are one of the few not disturbed, well, then you are one of the few! Isn't Yahweh NOT like the gods of the ancient world? Isn't Yahweh outraged by child sacrifice, having condemned it as a

---

3. Capon, *Kingdom, Grace, Judgment*, 5.

capital offense in Israel?[4] The answer, of course, is yes. What if, however, the text is divinely designed to be unsolvable, unanswerable, and incomplete in its original historical meaning? That is, what if it is a "stick figure"? What if the original historical meaning is initial but incomplete revelation to be completed by the arrival of the Bible's Superhero? If this is true, then it will certainly wake up our Bible reading!

Finally, the *Running Commentary* is also where the preacher blends personally discovered insights with the insights of others or study aids.[5] The significance of the *Running Commentary* lies in its interpretive powers. It forces an interpretation of the text toward its original historical meaning. In this way, the *Running Commentary* courageously moves beyond what the text says to what the text means. Therefore, the *Textual Map* combined with the *Running Commentary* furthers the discovery of the original historical meaning of the text. Together they impart the text's energies to you and through you to your listeners. In the Romans 10:1-4 example below, Main Ideas are italics, Supporting Idea(s) follow, and the Running Commentary is bulleted.

AN EXAMPLE FROM ROMANS 10:1-4

Main Idea #1: Israel is not achieving salvation or righteousness (v. 1).

Paul's passion is that they do (v. 1).
Paul prayer is that they do (v. 1).

- Verse 1 summarizes the substitutionary shaped heart of Paul from Romans 9:1-3.
- Verse 1 is literally translated, "Brothers the desire of my heart and my prayer to God on behalf of them (is) for salvation"—"on behalf of them" strikes a substitutionary tone.
- Paul's prayer is an "urgent request to meet a need, exclusively addressed to God" (BDAG).
- "Salvation" is a noun, not a verb—a desirable state, condition, or reality.

---

4. Leviticus 18:21, 20:2-5 and 1 Kings 11:7, 23:10 for starters.
5. Study aids are encouraged once the preacher has put some "sweat equity" in the text.

Main Idea #2: Israel struggles for righteousness (vv. 2-3).

Before God and his Law (v. 2).
Without understanding (v. 2).
Without understanding the righteousness from God (v. 3).
By seeking to establish a righteousness from human effort (v. 3).
By not submitting to the active power (force) of the righteousness from God (v. 3).

- The word "for" in v. 2 is a connector word explaining why Israel is falling short of salvation.
- Paul "bears witness" as an Apostle, that is, a divinely authorized official witness.
- "Zeal" means an "intense positive interest in something . . . marked by a sense of dedication" (BDAG). It also carries an element of "intense negative feelings" (BDAG) for its opposition. Therefore, Israel possessed intense passion and commitment to God and his Law and also intense intolerance for those who didn't.
- Their "zeal for God but not according to knowledge" means they are missing truth or reality as the proper object and/or source of their zeal. Zeal without knowledge is a narrative. It is fanaticism, extremism, and terrorism (see Saul prior to becoming Paul), not true devotion to God, justice, or righteousness. It also implies not really knowing God, justice, or righteousness.
- The word "for" in v. 3 is a connector word explaining what Israel is missing—the righteousness *from God*. God is a genitive of source or origin,[6] therefore, this is a righteousness *from God*. It is a received-righteousness, not an achieved-righteousness. It is a grace-righteousness, not a law-righteousness. It is a Jesus-righteousness, not a self-righteousness.
- The main verb in v. 3 is "they did not submit to the righteousness from God." "Submit" has two supporting ideas (participles) that explain why Israel did not submit to the righteousness from God: 1) they did not understand the righteousness from God (i.e., a grace-righteousness, received-righteousness, Jesus-righteousness), 2) they were seeking to establish their own righteousness (i.e., a law-righteousness, achieved-righteousness, self-righteousness).

---

6. Wallace, *Basics of New Testament Syntax*, 56.

Main Idea #3: *Christ is the end of the struggle for righteousness (v. 4).*

That is Christ has achieved law-righteousness.
That is the end of the struggle for law-righteousness is over.
That is for all who believe (v. 4).

- The word "for" in v. 4 is a connector word explaining why Israel's (everyone's) struggle for righteousness in v. 3 is over.

- Paul seems to employ six distinct meanings for "law" in his writings: 1) the law as the Old Testament, 2) the law as an era of salvation history, 3) the law as God's moral law for human flourishing (ten commandments), God's standards of righteousness and life, or as the spiritual fabric of the universe, 4) the law as a force or power, 5) the law as a principle, and 6) the law as a form of self-salvation, works-righteousness, legalism, system of salvation, or way to establish (achieve) a righteousness of your own. Christ brings an end to the law as a way to establish (achieve) a righteousness of your own. In other words, all the multi-form strategies of self-justification come to an end with a Jesus-justification.

- How does Christ bring an end to the law as a way to establish (achieve) a righteousness of one's own? The word "end" in verse 4 has three possible meanings according to Douglas Moo's commentary on Romans (pp. 640–1): 1) termination—Christ's person and work brings an end to the law in some manner, 2) goal—Christ's person and work fulfills the purpose or intent of the law in some manner, 3) result—Christ's person and work results in or produces the effects of the law in some manner. How is "end" being used in verse 4? The dynamics of salvation history are certainly in play in Romans, that is, the law as an era of salvation history and Jesus Christ as an era of salvation history. Therefore, the meaning could be Jesus brings an "end" to the law as an era of salvation history. The dynamics of personal salvation are also in play in Romans, that is, an individual sinner's justification, sanctification, glorification, or otherwise comprehensive salvation before God. Therefore, the meaning could be Jesus brings an "end" to the law to establish (achieve) a righteousness of your own before God (justification).

- Jesus is the only human being on the planet to achieve a law-righteousness before God, that is, to establish a righteousness of his own. Therefore, Jesus has done what Adam did not do. What Israel did not do. What no human being has been able to do—including me and my listeners.

- Why did God (Jesus) become a human being to establish (achieve) a righteousness of his own? Did Jesus need to establish a law-righteousness of his own for himself, that is, to fill up something lacking? Did Jesus need to justify himself, that is, his person and works for his sake? Of course not! But as Savior, Jesus came to establish (achieve) a law-righteousness for those who have none—the unrighteous in Romans 1–5. But as Savior, Jesus came so God could be both just and justifier (Rom 3:25–6; 4:5). Therefore, Jesus established a righteousness of his own (a law-righteousness) on behalf of those who have none, that is, for "everyone who believes."

- The phrase "everyone who believes" in v. 4 is an adjectival participle. It describes the person who receives the righteousness from God rather than seeks to establish (achieve) a righteousness of their own. In other words, the person who believes trusts in Jesus and his righteousness (faith) not in themselves and their own righteousness (works).

- The climax of Romans 10:1–4 is v. 4! The deep struggle for righteousness is finally over! The obsession to prove ourselves, be enough, do more, establish a righteousness of our own, justify our very existence, or avoid doom (the condemnation of our very being) is over. There is now justification and life in Jesus' person and righteousness. There is now peace and freedom because of Jesus and his work of salvation. Therefore, in Christ there is peace and freedom before God, the Law, ourselves, others, and all of life. In Christ, there is the peace and freedom of forgetting ourselves. In Christ, there is the peace and freedom of living outward in faith to God and love to neighbor. In Christ, there are no more trials, that is, that horrible feeling of being watched, measured, and judged by God, ourselves, others, the law of success, or the accusatory stare of bad "luck." In Christ, there is no more self-entanglement, hostile powers of condemnation, fear and anxiety, and all the multi-forms of doom from trying to establish (achieve) a righteousness of your own.

Chapter 7

Discover the Text's Message

Pole 1 of the Gospel Arc preaching model is the original historical meaning of a biblical text. In other words, the text's message. After doing the work to understand the text (Round 2), it is time to discover the text's living and active message (Round 3).

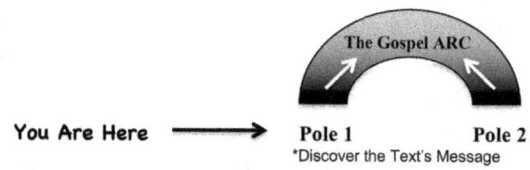

The Gospel Arc

ROUND 3: DISCOVER THE TEXT'S MESSAGE

1. Identify a particular aspect of the *Human Condition* (HC) addressed in the text (record in a sticky statement or vivid image):

Human Condition Tool (record in a sticky statement or vivid image):

- What is the *God-sized* or *God-shaped "hole"* found in the text due to the functional impact of the absence of God upon the human condition (i.e., the fallen condition is both deprived and depraved)?
- What is the *"mental map"* (way of seeing) and/or *"heart map"* (way of trusting) of the individual people and/or corporate people (culture) in the text?
- What is the universal human need, burden, condition, or conflict in or behind the text?
- Who are the *people* or what are the *places* in view in the text?
- What is the universal human condition of the participants and/or hearers being addressed?
- What required the writing of this text?
- Why might the Holy Spirit have inspired the text?
- What is the universal human need, burden, condition, or conflict in the text that requires the grace of Jesus Christ and his salvation?
- What are the *background beliefs* or *alternate beliefs* in the text that correspond to your hearers in order to *connect* (point of contact) and *challenge* (push on pressure point) and *re-connect* (re-enchant with the gospel)?
- What is the idol, god-replacement, substitute-savior, or self-salvation strategy in the text?

2. Identify the primary thing the text is *saying* or the *Big Idea* of the text.

Big Idea Tool (record in a sticky statement or vivid image):

- What is the primary powerful thing the text is *saying*?
- What is the dominant thought, idea, image, story, need, "Aha!," subject, theme, or content in the text?
- What is the "freshly squeezed" essence of the text?
- This text is about _____.
- The "Speech" in Speech-Act.

3. Identify the primary thing the text is *doing* with what it is saying or the *Applied Big Idea* of the text. Because God's Word *does* what it *says*!

Applied Big Idea Tool (record in a sticky statement or vivid image):

- What is the primary powerful thing the text is *doing* with what it is saying?
- Where is the passage *going*?
- Where is the passage *taking us*?
- What is the *"so what?"* force, function, movement, intention, action, practical difference, or transformative possibility of the controlling content?
- This text is doing _____.
- What are the energies being imparted by the text?
- The "Act" in Speech-Act.
- How the gospel re-enchants lives, relationships, communities, places, all of life (the world).

Literary Tool:

- If the text is *narrative literature* or a *story*, then discover how the setting, characters, conflict or plot line, and resolution or lack thereof communicate the three interpretive textual tracks (i.e., the human condition, Big Idea, and Applied Big Idea of the text).
- If the text is *propositional literature* or a *logical argument*, then discover how the flow of the main and supporting ideas communicate the three interpretive textual tracks.
- If the text is *law* or an *ethical principle*, then discover how the ideal or anti-ideal communicate the three interpretive textual tracks.
- If the text is *wisdom literature*, then discover how the *fabric of creation* (i.e., the regular patterns or order in creation) or the *futility of creation* (i.e., the irregular patterns or active de-creation because of sin in creation) communicates the three interpretive textual tracks.

- If the text is *poetic literature*, then discover how the image that brings the *world of proposition* and the *world of sensory experience* together communicates the three interpretive textual tracks.
- If the text is *apocalyptic literature*, then discover how the visual revelation (rather than aural) communicates the three interpretive textual tracks.

INSTRUCTION

The aim of discovering the original historical message of the text is to identify three interpretive textual tracks that mutually inform each other :

1. The specific aspect of the human condition being addressed in the text.
2. The dominate thing the text is saying or a Big Idea of the text.
3. The dominate thing the text is doing with what it is saying, or an Applied Big Idea of the text.

A sermon message of the text is discovered by either blending these three interpretive textual tracks together to form one sticky statement, vivid image, or suspenseful question, or by identifying one that rules them all while the others play supporting roles. At this point, however, record and work with each of the three interpretive textual tracks separately, thereby crafting a sticky statement or vivid image for each:

1. The specific aspect of the *human condition* being addressed in the text.
2. The dominate thing the text is saying or a *Big Idea* of the text.
3. The dominate thing the text is doing with what it is saying, or an *Applied Big Idea* of the text.

Discover the Human Condition of the Text

To discover the specific facet of the human condition being addressed in the text, it is helpful to answer one or more of the following questions of the text (record answer in a sticky statement or vivid image):

- What is the *God-sized* or *God-shaped* "hole" found in the text due to the functional impact of the absence of God upon the human condition (i.e., the fallen condition is both deprived of God and depraved by sin)?

- What is the *"mental map"* (way of seeing) and/or *"heart map"* (way of trusting) of the individual people and/or corporate people (culture) in the text?
- What is the universal human need, burden, condition, or conflict in or behind the text?
- Who are the *people* or what are the *places* in view in the text?
- What is the universal human condition of the participants and/or hearers being addressed?
- What required the writing of this text?
- Why might the Holy Spirit have inspired the text?
- What is the universal human need, burden, condition, or conflict in the text that requires the grace of Jesus Christ and his salvation?
- What are the *background beliefs* or *alternate beliefs* in the text that correspond to your hearers in order to connect (point of contact) and challenge (push on pressure point) and ultimately re-connect (re-enchant with the gospel)?[1]
- What is the *idol*, god-replacement, substitute-savior, or self-salvation strategy in the text?

Let's expand a few ways to discover the human condition in the text. The "go to" way in any given text is the *God-sized* or *God-shaped hole* in the soul.[2] The text might address the justification-shaped *hole in the soul*, that is, the "legal hole in the soul" before God which simultaneously reaches the deepest roots of one's being. Therefore, even for the Christian, the need to functionally experience justification by faith in this and that area of one's life and relationships is ongoing. It is the engine of sanctification.

For example, Jesus is prompted by the condition of the lawyer's heart to tell the story of the "Good Samaritan": "But he, desiring to justify himself, said to Jesus, 'And who is my neighbor?'" (Luke 10:29). The lawyer has a justification-shaped hole in his soul (legally and existentially), that is, he is desperate to prove himself. Sound familiar? Most garden-variety sins (i.e., not being a good neighbor, lying, selfishness, anger, defensiveness, anxiety), as well as the more notorious ones (i.e., murder, theft, racism, violence, narcissism, pathologies, addictions, evil acts of control), flow from the polluted

---

1. Keller and Clowney, "Preaching Christ in a Postmodern World."
2. God even dedicated a whole book of Bible (Ecclesiastes) to address the divine hole in the soul of meaninglessness, emptiness, or nothingness that is the result of alienation from God.

spring of self-justification. When we *functionally* trust in race, power, control, human approval, a political ideology, our performance, the law of success and failure, accomplishments (or lack thereof), the law of body image, being a good person, ministry, etc., to justify or doom our existence, we *do* whatever the god requires.

Another way to approach the human condition in the text is to explore its *mental map*, that is, the thinking and feeling of the people and culture in the text as well as its original recipients. How did they see the world? What was their lens or interpretation of reality, that is, of God, others, themselves, their circumstances, relationships, money, sex, suffering, justice, evil, identity, family, and so on?

For example, Martha has a *mental map* about Jesus, "Lord, do you not care that my sister has left me to serve alone? Tell her to help me" (Luke 10:40). Jesus addresses her messy mental map by saying, "Martha, Martha, you are anxious and troubled about many things, but one thing is necessary. Mary has chosen the good portion, which will not be taken from her" (Luke 10:41). Obviously, the *mental map* and *heart map* work together to reveal two sides of the one inner person—their thinking/feeling and trusting.

What required the writing of this text? and *Why might the Holy Spirit have inspired this text?* are probes into the human condition not only of the original participants in the text,[3] but also of the original recipients of the text. For example, Paul wrote Galatians to address specific aspects of the human condition found in "the churches of Galatia" (Gal 1:2). Therefore, pressing into the Galatian human condition reveals what required the writing of the text and, thereby, what hooks the contemporary human heart as well. In this way, discovering the Galatian human condition prepares you and your listeners for the divine energies of the gospel released in the book of Galatians.

Discovering the *background beliefs* and *alternate beliefs* in the text help identify fixed beliefs of unbelief not only found in the text but also in your listeners and the culture around them. For example, modern people still seek human wisdom in all its multi-forms (i.e., reason and science) just like the Greeks in an attempt to control their lives (1 Cor 1–2). Religious people (including evangelicals) still seek power in all its multi-forms (i.e., spiritual and political) just like the Jews in an obsession to self-improve. Once you've identified a fixed belief of unbelief, Tim Keller's rapid apologetic approach[4] is helpful: 1) *connect* to the universal human condition—

---

3. Like the lawyer Jesus tells the "Good Samaritan" story too, or the actual characters in the "Good Samaritan" story (i.e., man who fell among robbers, the robbers, priest, Levite, Samaritan, innkeeper, et al.).

4. Keller and Clowney, "Preaching Christ in a Postmodern World."

"we all struggle to control our lives," 2) *challenge* the broken ways we try to address our human condition—"our need to control controls us," and 3) *re-connect* to the only One who can address our human condition—"Jesus is all the control you need."

Discover the *Big Idea* of the Text

To discover a *Big Idea* of the text, it is helpful to answer at least one of the following questions of the text:

1. What is one powerful thing the text is saying?
2. What is a dominant thought, idea, image, story, need, "Aha!" moment, subject, theme, or content in the text?
3. What is the freshly squeezed essence of the text?
4. This text is about _____.
5. The "Speech" in Speech-Act.

Discovering a *Big Idea* of the text requires courage. Even if it feels like Custer's last stand, you must take an interpretive stand. Therefore, fill in the blank: This text is about _____." This is your *Big Idea*.

You must put behind you the pressure (and debate?) of locating one lone single divinely inspired right Big Idea in the text. Bravely push forward and answer: *What is one powerful thing the text is saying?* Don't be a wimp. Need some courage? Luther can help, "the power of Scripture is this: it will not be altered by the one who studies it; instead, it transforms the one who loves it. It draws the individual in—into itself—and into its own powers."[5]

Also, the *Big Idea* is the "Speech" in Speech-Act,[6] that is, it is dominating speech or content in a particular passage. It is what God is primarily *saying* in a text. Therefore, seek to discover God's primary "Speech" in a text. How? Start with words, ideas, images, repetitions, stories, characters, actions, events, places, and more. Learn how the literary form of the text you are working with helps communicate Big Ideas (see below). At its most fundamental level, the *Big Idea* is routinely discovered by literally or intuitively itemizing main and supporting ideas in the text—and then by identifying one that rules them all. Therefore ask, *what is the dominant thought, idea,*

---

5. Quoted in Bayer, *Martin Luther's Theology*, 71.

6. See Chapter 12 for further development of the Bible as a Divine "Speech-Act," that is, God's Word does what it says.

image, story, need, "Aha!" moment, subject, theme, or *content* in the text? The answer is your *Big Idea*.

Discover the *Applied Big Idea* of the Text

To discover an *Applied Big Idea* of the text, it is helpful to answer one or more of the following questions of the text (record answers in a sticky statement or vivid image):

1. What is one powerful thing the text is doing with what it is saying?
2. Where is the passage going?
3. Where is the passage taking the reader?
4. What is the force, function, movement, intention, action, practical difference, or transformative possibility of the controlling content?
5. This text is doing _____.
6. What are the energies being imparted by the text?
7. What is the "Act" in Speech-Act?
8. How does the gospel re-enchant lives, relationships, communities, places, all of life (the world)?

Discovering an *Applied Big Idea* of the text pushes beyond what the text is *saying* (i.e., the Big Idea) to what the text is *doing* with what it is saying. Therefore, fill in the blank: *The text is doing* ___. This is your *Applied Big Idea*.

Push deep into your bones that the text is *doing* something. It is *going* somewhere. It is getting something *done*, not just conveying information.[7] Therefore, ask, *What is the text doing? Where is the text going? What is the text getting done?* The answer is your *Applied Big Idea*.

Many call the *Applied Big Idea* the "so what?" or the practical application of the text or Big Idea. While this is true, the point is not coming up (each week) with creative and relevant applications for your listeners, which if we're honest, most of us, well, suck at. Rather, tap into the text's own energies and power. In other words, the text is already *doing something* apart from you (and your creative relevant applications). It is living and active. It is releasing the personal active presence of the Word Himself into lives, relationships, and the world. Therefore, *what are the energies being imparted by the text?* The answer is your *Applied Big Idea*.

---

7. Keller, *Prayer: Experiencing Awe and Intimacy with God*, 52.

Furthermore, the *Applied Big Idea* is the "Act" in Speech-Act,[8] that is, the dominating action in a particular passage. It is what God is primarily *doing* in a text. Therefore, seek to discover God's primary "Act" in a text. How? Start with words, ideas, images, repetitions, stories, characters, actions, events, places, and more. Learn how the literary form of the text you are working with helps communicate Applied Big Ideas (see below). At its most fundamental level, the *Applied Big Idea* is routinely discovered by identifying what the Big Idea of the text is *doing*. Therefore, ask, What is the force, function, movement, intention, action, practical difference, or transformative possibility of the Big Idea in the text? The answer is your *Applied Big Idea*.

Also, since the gospel of Jesus and his salvation re-enchants lives, relationships, communities, places, all of life (the world), look for this re-enchantment in the text. Ask, *How does the gospel re-enchant lives, relationships, communities, places, all of life (the world) in this text?* The answer is your *Applied Big Idea*. Perhaps in many texts, there is also the noticeable absence or lack of gospel re-enchantment. Then look for the *Applied Big Idea* in its absence.

Take Note of the Literary Form of the Text

Further resources to help discover the three interpretive textual tracks (i.e., the human condition, Big Idea, and Applied Big Idea) can be found in the literary form of the text. For example:

- If the text is narrative literature or a story, then discover how the setting, characters, conflict or plot line, and resolution or lack thereof communicate the three interpretive textual tracks.

- If the text is propositional literature or a logical argument, then discover how the flow of the main and supporting ideas communicate the three interpretive textual tracks.

- If the text is law or an ethical principle, then discover how the ideal or anti-ideal communicate the three interpretive textual tracks.

- If the text is wisdom literature, then discover how the *fabric of creation* (i.e., the regular patterns or order of creation) or the *futility of creation* (i.e., the irregular patterns or active de-creation because of sin in creation) communicate the three interpretive textual tracks.

---

8. See Chapter 12 for further development of the Bible as a Divine "Speech-Act," that is, God's Word does what it says.

- If the text is poetic literature, then discover how the image that brings the world of proposition and the world of sensory experience together communicate the three interpretive textual tracks.
- If the text is apocalyptic literature, then discover how the visual revelation (rather than aural) communicates the three interpretive textual tracks.

Let's take Psalm 88 as an example of how poetic literature can communicate the three interpretive tracks of the *human condition*, *Big Idea*, and *Applied Big Idea* in the text. Psalm 88 is the gloomy Psalm. Reading it can be terrifying: "Welcome to hell on earth . . ." It is one gruesome image after another itemizing the devastating aspects of spiritual depression.

Therefore, the images communicate the *human condition*: spiritual depression is devastating. The sheer number and magnitude of these images also reveal the *Big Idea*. Therefore, recorded in the form of a suspenseful question, the *Big Idea* might be: How devastating is spiritual depression? The answers become movements for a sermon map:[9] You feel dead, your body just hasn't figured it out yet (vv. 3–5, 11–12). You feel all alone, with people all around you (vv. 8, 18). You feel actively abandoned by God (vv. 14, 6–8, 17–18, and 13).[10]

What about the *Applied Big Idea* for Psalm 88? Verse 1 is the torch we are intended to take into the cave of Psalm 88: "O Lord, God of my salvation." Therefore, Psalm 88 begins the dark journey into the cave of spiritual depression by *doing something*. What is it *doing*? The answer is giving you a torch, the torch of salvation! The torch of a God who descends into death with you and for you on the cross. The torch of a God who actively abandons himself on the cross so he doesn't have to abandon you. Take the torch of God's salvation into your cave.[11]

In sum, Pole 1 is the first component of the Gospel Arc preaching model. It is the original historical meaning of the biblical text. It is the text's message or what the passage is *saying* (Big Idea) and *doing* (Applied Big Idea) in its original historical context. The aim of Pole 1 is to discover the original historical meaning of the biblical text by: 1) listening to the text, 2) understanding the text, and 3) discovering the message of the text. Discovering the message of the text involves three interpretive textual tracks that mutually inform each other: 1) a specific human condition revealed in the

---

9. See "Round 5: Crafting a Sermon Message" for more coverage of a Sermon Map.

10. The order of these verses reflect possible movements in a sermon map.

11. The torch of v. 1 is a solid gospel thread leading to Jesus and his salvation. See "Round 4: Discover the Textual Jesus" for more coverage on how to follow a gospel thread to Jesus.

text, 2) the Big Idea or what the text is saying, 3) and the Applied Big Idea or what the text is doing with what it is saying. The final product for Pole 1 of the Gospel Arc preaching model is three sticky statements or vivid images, one for each of the following:

1. The specific aspect of the human condition being addressed in the text.
2. The primary thing the text is saying or the Big Idea of the text.
3. The primary thing the text is doing with what it is saying or the Applied Big Idea of the text.

AN EXAMPLE FROM ROMANS 10:1–4

The Human Condition

The deep struggle for righteousness.

This *Human Condition* is the result of asking and answering, "What is the universal human need, burden, condition, or conflict in the text that requires the grace of Jesus Christ and his salvation?"

The Big Idea

The end of the struggle for righteousness.

This *Big Idea* is the result of filling in the blank: This text is about _____.

The Applied Big Idea

End your struggle for righteousness.

This *Applied Big Idea* is the result of asking and answering, "What is one powerful thing the text is doing with what it is saying?"

Chapter 8

Discover the Textual Jesus

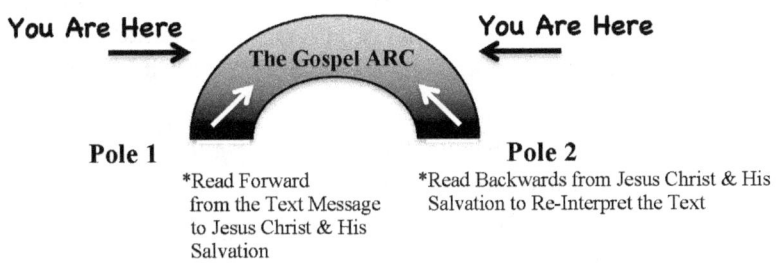

The Gospel Arc

Pole 2 is the second component of the Gospel Arc preaching model. Pole 2 is Jesus Christ and his salvation, which is the ultimate revelatory lens for reading the Bible, the climax of God's revelation, the ultimate message of the Bible, the redemptive-historical meaning of the original historical text, and the ultimate message of a specific text to reach and renew lives, relationships, communities, and the world.

Pole 2 changes everything, including how to read the Bible. Pole 2 retrospectively rereads, re-narrates, or reinterprets all previous revelation. Pole 2 involves, fulfills, escalates, corresponds to, completes, addresses, satisfies, perfects, resolves, or maps more meaning onto all previous revelation.

Therefore, a biblical text has not been properly understood, applied, or communicated until its message (Pole 1) has been integrated with the overall message of the Bible culminating in Jesus Christ and his salvation (Pole 2). That is, with the *Textual Jesus*.

The aim of connecting or integrating Pole 1 to Pole 2 of the Gospel Arc preaching model is to craft a specific *Textual Jesus* to build the sermon around. In other words, the aim is to experience Jesus with the Bible by faith to reach and renew the world (Rom 1:16).

ROUND 4: DISCOVER THE TEXTUAL JESUS

1. *Read forward* by following the divinely embedded *Gospel Threads* in the text. These threads carry a *surplus of meaning*. Follow these gospel threads to their ultimate end in Jesus Christ and his salvation (think it out below).

Gospel Thread Tool (Pole 1 gives a *pattern of significance* to Jesus Christ and his salvation):

- An **attribute and/or action of God** in the text that is addressing the universal human condition, need, or burden in the text. Follow this gospel thread to its ultimate example or embodiment in Jesus Christ and his salvation.
- A **theme or idea** in the text. Follow this gospel thread to its ultimate resolution in Jesus Christ and his salvation.
- A **law or biblical ethic** in the text. Follow this gospel thread to its completion in Jesus Christ and his salvation.
- An **image** in the text. Follow this gospel thread to its ultimate target in Jesus Christ and his salvation.
- A **type or pattern** in the text. Follow this gospel thread to its ultimate fulfillment, substance, or perfection in Jesus Christ and his salvation.
- A **story of an individual or community** in the text. Follow this gospel thread to its ultimate bigger story of Jesus Christ and his salvation.
- An **instinct or sense** in the text. Follow this gospel thread to its ultimate convergence on Jesus Christ and his salvation.
- A **sin and its consequences**, a *heart and life issue*, a *cultural heart and life issue*, a *spiritual need*, a *universal human "hole," condition, burden, and problem* in the text.

- The **human longing in the text**. Follow this gospel thread to its ultimate satisfaction in Jesus Christ and his salvation.
- The **functional human trust**, hope, love, worship, salvation, justification, or God-replacement in the text. Follow this gospel thread to its ultimate source and satisfaction in Jesus Christ and his salvation.
- The **grace at work in the text**. Follow this gospel thread to its ultimate source in Jesus Christ and his salvation.

2. *Read backwards* by looking through the *Gospel Lens* to re-interpret or find the *surplus of meaning* in the text (think it out below).

Gospel Lens Tool (Pole 2 *maps more meaning* onto, completes, or reinterprets Pole 1).

Look at how Jesus and his salvation:

- Address the universal human need, condition, or burden in the text.
- Solve tensions in the text.
- Accomplish what the text is doing (i.e., the ultimate application of the text).
- Involve, correspond to, map more meaning onto, fulfill, escalate, or complete the signifiers (gospel threads) in the text.
- Interpret the Old Testament allusions, echoes, or quotations in the New Testament text.
- Provide the source or ultimate work of grace in the text.

3. Craft the specific *Textual Jesus* in the text into *one* sticky statement or vivid image (this freshly crafted *Textual Jesus* is what the sermon is built around):

Textual Jesus Tool:

- Connect Pole 1 and Pole 2 to each other to form a **Gospel Arc**. This is your *Textual Jesus*.
- Take 2 lumps of clay (Pole 1 and Pole 2) and craft ONE specific aspect of Jesus Christ and his salvation from the text.

- What is a specific aspect of Jesus Christ and his salvation in the text to reach and renew lives, relationships, places, the world?
- Locate the Jesus of the text or the Word in the Word.

INSTRUCTION

There are two ways to connect or integrate the text (Pole 1) to Jesus Christ and his salvation (Pole 2), and the meaning flows both ways:

1. Read forward from the text to Jesus Christ and his salvation.
2. Read backwards from Jesus Christ and his salvation to the text.

Read Forward

The key to reading forward is finding and following the gospel thread(s) in the text that lead to Jesus Christ and his salvation. A gospel thread not only signifies itself in the text but also connects to Jesus Christ and his salvation. Therefore, a gospel thread is loaded with a surplus of meaning beyond its original historical meaning. Discovering the gospel thread(s) in the text connects the text (Pole 1) to Jesus Christ and his salvation (Pole 2).

How does one discover the gospel threads in the text? There are many biblical ways to find potential gospel threads in a text.[1] The Gospel Arc preaching model begins the search for gospel threads in the text's message or the three interpretive tracks discovered in Round 3: 1) a specific aspect of the human condition in the text, 2) the Big Idea of the text, and 3) the Applied Big Idea of the text. Read forward from the text's message (the three interpretive tracks) to Jesus and his salvation. Discover and follow these potential gospel threads to their ultimate example, embodiment, act, accomplishment, resolution, completion, target, perfection, convergence, solution, satisfaction, or source in Jesus Christ and his salvation:[2]

- An attribute and/or action of God in the text that is addressing the universal human condition, need, or burden in the text.

---

1 Some helpful Christocentric preaching resources to discover potential gospel threads in the text are: Chapell, *Christ-Centered Preaching*; Goldsworthy, *Preaching the Whole Bible as Christian Scripture*; Greidanus, *Preaching Christ from the Old Testament*; Keller, *Preaching* and *Center Church*; Miller and Campbell, *Saving Eutychus: How to Preach God's Word and Keep People Awake*.

2. See Keller, *Preaching*, 70–90, for a more thorough look at potential gospel threads.

- A theme or idea in the text.
- A law or biblical ethic in the text.
- An image in the text.
- A type or pattern in the text.
- A story of an individual or community in the text.
- An instinct or sense in the text.
- A sin and its consequences, a heart and life issue, a cultural heart and life issue, a spiritual need, a universal human "hole," condition, burden, and problem in the text.
- The universal human longing in the text.
- The functional human trust, hope, love, worship, salvation, justification, or God-replacement in the text.
- The grace at work in the text.

Let's look at a few gospel threads or how to read forward.[3] The Old Testament, obviously, overflows with *attributes and actions of God*. In other words, God's worth and work. The Apostle John tells us, "No one has ever seen God; the only God (the Word or Jesus), who is at the Father's side, he has made him known" (John 1:18). And the Apostle Paul tells us, "He [Jesus] is the image of the invisible God (Col 1:15)." Both John and Paul say Jesus reveals God not only because he himself is God, but also because he is the ultimate exegesis or interpretation of God. Jesus' worth and work narrates the invisible God for us (John 1:14–18). Therefore, the visible attributes and actions of God in the Old Testament are gospel threads that inherently connect to Jesus and his salvation, that is, the image of the invisible God.

How do you practically read forward from an Old Testament *attribute and action of God* to a New Testament Jesus? After completing "Round 3: Discover the Text's Message" of the Gospel Arc preaching method, you will have in your possession a specific aspect of the human condition recorded either as a sticky statement or a vivid image. Now ask, what *attribute and action of God* is revealed in this text (perhaps context) to address this human condition, need, or burden in the text? The answer is your gospel thread to Jesus and his salvation.

For example, in Numbers 13, God instructs Moses to send out twelve spies into Canaan to bring back some good news to energize faith in Israel. Instead, they bring back a "bad report" (v. 32) crammed with inferior

---

3. Certainly, some gospel threads or ways to read forward will overlap at times. When they do, pick the one that most moves you!

"grasshoppers" and superior "giants"—all likely places for the human condition to hide. Caleb and Joshua, two spiritual celebrities, rush to stop Israel's panic attack. They address Israel's need to see something else: "The Lord is with us" (Num 14:9). Therefore, follow Caleb and Joshua's *attribute and action of God* (gospel thread) to Jesus, "Immanuel," or "God with us" (Matt 1:23). In this way, Jesus is so with us that he entered the land of the Dark Powers on the cross to get us (Col 2:11–15). In this way, Jesus identifies with spiritual grasshoppers to the point that he actually became one, disarming all the spiritual giants against you (Col 2:11–15).

Themes, ideas, laws, and *biblical ethics* are obviously present in both the Old and New Testament. Therefore, start with those that travel or exist in both. Why? Because they must be pretty significant if they show up in both places!

For example, look for the *themes* or *ideas* of creation, new creation, kingdom, covenant, home, exile, light, darkness, rest, work, slave, son, slavery, redemption, justification, condemnation, nakedness, clothing, judgment, salvation, weakness, power, shame, honor, fear, faith, rejection, love, and more that traverse the Bible from cover to cover. Look for the *law* or *biblical ethic* of loving God and neighbor, the Ten Commandments as the spiritual fabric of the universe and humanity and, thereby, the source and dynamic of human flourishing (individually and corporately), and the myriad applications for loving God and others, and more that crisscross the Bible.[4]

For a *theme* or *idea*, follow this gospel thread to its ultimate resolution in Jesus and his salvation. For example, nakedness in the Bible begins with the tension of being naked before God, others, ourselves, the Law, and the endless little laws of life (like being a good mom), and ends in the terror of terminal condemnation and shame. No wonder being watched or looked at is uncomfortable. No wonder there is such a thing as "performance anxiety" and the growing demand for mental health experts. Therefore, follow the gospel thread of nakedness to its resolution in Jesus and his salvation. That is, Jesus stripped naked on the cross for us. Jesus absorbed all our condemnation and shame on the cross. Jesus cloths us with his own achieved-righteousness. Nakedness is clothed or resolved in Jesus.

For a *law* or *biblical ethic*, follow this gospel thread to its ultimate completion in Jesus and his salvation. For example, loving God and neighbor begins in the Bible as a righteous and flourishing outward-directed life

---

4. Note that laws and biblical ethics may appear in their ideal or anti-ideal form. And also in a variety of shapes and sizes: characters or figures (hearts, lives, behavior, relationships), settings (backgrounds), actions, events, institutions, imperatives (commands), indicatives (portrayals of reality), stories, wisdom sayings, images, etc.

on all fronts—spiritually, psychologically, relationally, vocationally, and culturally—that quickly disappears into the darkness of self (Gen 3). Therefore, follow the gospel thread of loving God and neighbor to its ultimate completion in Jesus and his salvation. That is, Jesus loved God and neighbor perfectly for those imprisoned in themselves. Jesus was cursed on the cross for those terminally curved in on themselves. Jesus became enslaved to sin to set us free to love God and others. Loving God and neighbor is completed in Jesus.

For an *image*, follow this gospel thread to its ultimate target in Jesus and his salvation. Images can be people, places, actions, events, institutions, impersonal objects, creatures, symbols, themes and ideas, and more. In other words, they can be just about anything! Since anything in life can be used to communicate thoughts and feelings about something else, do four things: 1) identity the image in the text, 2) locate its target in the text, 3) attach its thoughts and feelings to the target, and 4) connect those thoughts and feelings to the ultimate target of Jesus and his salvation.

For example, "The Lord is my shepherd" (Ps 23:1). The image is "shepherd"; the target is "Lord." Possible thoughts and feelings of "shepherd" to be attached to Lord might be the personal active presence of God for his people, especially in dark places (v. 4). Now, follow the gospel thread of shepherd to its ultimate target of Jesus and his salvation. Jesus actually does it for us as he intentionally steps into Psalm 23, "I am the good shepherd . . . and I lay my life down for the sheep" (John 10:14–15). Connect the thoughts and feelings of the Psalm 23 shepherd to Jesus and his salvation. In this way, Jesus' death releases the personal active presence of God in the darkest hearts, lives, relationships, and places. Shepherd finds its ultimate target in Jesus and his salvation.

For a *type* or *pattern*, follow this gospel thread to its ultimate fulfillment, substance, or perfection in Jesus and his salvation. A *type* or *pattern* can include people, places, actions, events, institutions, impersonal objects, creatures, symbols, themes and ideas, and more just like an *image* (see above). Keep in mind, however, that the movement of a *type or pattern* is from stick figure to superhero, skeleton to completed body, shadow to substance, type to archetype, or pattern to perfection.

For example, the bronze serpent in the wilderness (Num 21:4–9). The human heart is poisoned with sin. Sometimes being told isn't enough; we must *feel* it. Therefore, God sends poisonous serpents into Israel to make sin real, and it works. Moses intercedes for Israel and God has mercy on them. How? By way of a bronze serpent. Why a bronze serpent? Because Israel needed a substitute serpent, death, or poison to be healed. All who looked upon the substitute serpent lived. Connect the gospel thread of the bronze serpent to Jesus and his salvation. Again, Jesus actually does it for us: "And as Moses lifted up the serpent in the wilderness, so must the Son of Man be lifted up, that whoever believes in him may have eternal life" (John 3:14).[5] Jesus takes the place of the poisoned person. Jesus becomes the cursed. Jesus becomes the walking dead. Jesus becomes the serpent. The pattern of the bronze serpent finds its ultimate perfection in Jesus and his salvation.

For the *story of an individual or community*, follow this gospel thread to its ultimate bigger story in Jesus and his salvation. Stories include characters (individuals and communities), places (settings), actions (events), storylines (drama), and endings (resolution or lack of). Pay attention to these story elements because they not only tell the original historical story, but also contribute patterns of significance (gospel threads) to the bigger story of Jesus and his salvation.

Take, for example, the famous David and Goliath story (1 Sam 17). Saul, who was king and the tallest figure in Israel, was called to be Israel's champion, that is, God's undefeatable savior who fights for Israel. Even Goliath, the Philistines' undefeated giant, knew this. He said so—two times a day for forty days—eighty times for those counting. But strangely, so did a nobody of a boy named David. So, while Saul and Israel watch and tremble in their utter inability to save themselves from Goliath, the Lord's newly anointed nobody (1 Sam 16) fights for Israel. He wins, of course, but with shocking ease. David's victory was Israel's victory, so Israel "rose with a shout" (1 Sam 17:52).

The bigger story of Jesus and his salvation is easily recognized once we quit drawing that first hermeneutical line from David to us. Taking Jesus with you to read the Bible changes everything. Jesus becomes the Lord's undefeatable Champion! Jesus now fights for you! And we, if we are anybody in the story, are like Saul and Israel trembling at our utter inability to save ourselves from even bigger giants than Goliath. Therefore, we, like Saul and Israel, watch in wonder as Someone fights for us. We, like Israel, rise with new life in the victory of Another. The story of David and Goliath is historically and hermeneutically connected to the bigger story of Jesus and his salvation.

For an *instinct*, follow this gospel thread to its ultimate convergence in Jesus and his salvation. *Instinct* is the Bible's Sixth Sense on steroids! It is seeing dead people everywhere! In other words, it is a way of seeing. It is a lens; it is intuitive; it is a gospel sense. It is what happens when Jesus and

---

5. Did Moses know the bronze serpent was a type or pattern of Jesus? Hardly. But God did. What Moses knew was true, but not exhaustive. In other words, God is a meaningful author of the Bible.

his salvation *is* the ultimate Subject (or Speech-Act) of the Bible. Keller says *instinct* is what happens when "you just can't not see him" in the Bible.[6]

For example, let's take an easy passage (I'm being facetious) like Romans 9, arguably, the most controversial chapter in all the Bible. For many, it is the last place to look for Jesus. But curiously, Paul begins this controversial passage by saying, "For I could wish that I myself were accursed and cut off from Christ for the sake of my brothers, my kinsmen according to the flesh" (v. 3). Breathtaking. "Oh God! Take me instead!" For my wife and kids, I might feel this way, but certainly not for a stranger. What's happening? The answer is at the very beginning of the chapter, where Paul gives the controlling lens by which to see the rest—a substitutionary heart. In other words, a substitutionary heart drives Romans 9, not a cold one. This is an *Instinct*. Follow the gospel thread of Paul's substitutionary heart to Jesus and his salvation. Therefore, what Paul wished, Jesus actually did. Paul wished he could be cut off for his brothers . . . Jesus was. If we walk away from Romans 9 ready to argue, then we don't get Romans 9. The amazing substitutionary love of Jesus drives the wonders of this passage.

In sum, Pole 1 reads forward or follows a *gospel thread* in the text to its ultimate end (or *telos*) in Jesus Christ and his salvation. Pole 1 gives a pattern of significance to Jesus Christ and his salvation in the text. This gospel thread leads to a *Textual Jesus* to be experienced by faith. Taking Jesus with you in preaching changes everything.

Read Backwards

The key to reading backwards is looking through the ultimate revelatory lens of Jesus Christ and his salvation (a gospel lens) to see or interpret the text in its new revelatory light. It is important to remember that Pole 2 is not disconnected from the original historical meaning of the text.[7] Rather, it is the ultimate historical and redemptive context and meaning of the text. Therefore, Pole 2 completes the Gospel ARC preaching model hermeneutically, biblically-theologically, and homiletically.

How does one look through the gospel lens of Jesus Christ and his salvation to reread or reinterpret the text? There are many ways to look

---

6. Keller, *Preaching: Communicating Faith in an Age of Skepticism*, 87.

7. The human author only view (liberal view), the divine author only view (allegorical view), and the divinely-inspired human author only view (evangelical view) of biblical authorship and authorial intent do not hermeneutically connect the original historical meaning of a biblical text to Jesus Christ and his salvation to enable the reader to understand, apply, and communicate the biblical text.

through a gospel lens to see the text.[8] The Gospel Arc suggests looking through the gospel lens to reread the text by seeing how Jesus Christ and his salvation:

1. Address the universal human need, condition, or burden in the text.
2. Address what the text is saying (i.e., the ultimate *Big Idea* of the text).
3. Accomplish what the text is doing (i.e., the ultimate *Applied Big Idea* of the text).
4. Solve tensions in the text.
5. Involve, correspond to, map more meaning onto, fulfill, escalate, or complete the signifiers (gospel threads) in the text.
6. Interpret the Old Testament allusions, echoes, or quotations in the New Testament text.
7. Provide the source or ultimate work of grace in the text.

Reading backwards is looking through the divinely provided revelatory lens of the gospel (Pole 2) to understand, apply, and communicate the biblical text (Pole 1). Pole 2 maps more meaning onto, completes, rereads, or reinterprets Pole 1. It sees the gospel threads in the text (Pole 1). It sees the embedded patterns of significance in the text. It sees the surplus of meaning in the text (Pole 1). Pole 2 is the Bible's Sixth Sense.

Let's look at a few ways to look through a *gospel lens* at the text to see more or to read backwards. After "Round 3: Discover the Text's Message," you will have recorded sticky statements or vivid images for the human condition, the Big Idea, and the Applied Big Idea of the text. Now, look at how Jesus and his salvation (the gospel lens) addresses them.

For example, if the *human condition* in Romans 10:1–4 is "the struggle for righteousness," then looking through a *gospel lens* ends the struggle (v. 4). If a *Big Idea* in Luke 7:1–10 is the suspenseful question, "What is God doing in your fear?" then looking through a *gospel lens* answers, "Leading you to the wonder of faith" (v. 9). If an *Applied Big Idea* in Mark 4:31–35 is, "Rest in the great care and calm of Jesus," then looking through a *gospel lens* sees more to the storm story. It sees a better Jonah resting perfectly in God amidst the storm for those who do not. It sees a better Jonah whose great care throws him overboard to stop the storm for those lost at sea. It sees a better Jonah whose great calm stops the greater storm of sin, death, and evil. Reading backwards looks at the text and your work in the text with a

---

8. Helpful Christocentric preaching resources for looking through a gospel lens to retrospectively re-interpret the text are Hays, *Echoes of Scripture in the Gospels* and *Echoes of Scripture in the Letters of Paul*.

gospel lens to see more. The *gospel lens* re-reads the text and, in so doing, sees more. It sees what's already there—originally—but now sees the surplus of meaning embedded in the text, retrospectively, through the gospel lens of Jesus and his salvation.

Another way to look at the text through a *gospel lens* is to *solve tensions* in the text with Jesus and his salvation. For example, the tension is rarely tighter than a God who doesn't care for us. The first recorded words of the disciples in the Gospel of Mark are, "Teacher, do you not care that we are perishing?" (Mark 4:38). These words are a big deal. They are primal words, first spoken besides a tree in paradise. They are primal words, simply waiting for a trigger to surge out of our own mouths. They are primal words that strike at the heart of who God is and Christianity. Answering wrongly will ruin you and your relationships. However, looking through a *gospel lens* at such high stakes tension does something. It allows us to see Jesus' answer. "Do I care? Do . . . I . . . care?" Jesus responds. Shaking off his sleepy slumber, Jesus verbally acts, speaking to the storm, "Quiet! Be still and stay still!" And the wind ceased, and there was a great calm (v. 39). Looking through a *gospel lens* we recognize, THAT was nothing! And we feel his greater care and greater calm at the cross and resurrection. Jesus really does answer this primal question of life.

If you are working with a New Testament text and find an *Old Testament allusion, echo,* or *quotation*, re-read it through a *gospel lens*. For example, Mark 4:38 says, "Do you not care that we are perishing?" These words are remarkably similar to the captain's words in Jonah, as he appeals to the care of God in a storm to prevent from perishing. And Mark 4:41 says, "And they were filled with great fear and said to one another . . ." This is a direct Hebrew description straight from Jonah—employed twice (1:10 and 1:16). When we re-read these *Old Testament allusions, echoes,* or *quotations* through a *gospel lens*, we see a bigger and better Jonah Story.

Wherever *grace* is found in the Bible, somehow it is always strange, surprising, odd, unexpected, incomprehensible, not normal, not natural, bizarre, astonishing, foreign, mysterious, unknown, unfathomable, extraordinary, or remarkable. In other words, it is inexplicably *grace*. *Grace* can only show up in the Bible, hearts, lives, words, behavior, actions, relationships, home, work, church, communities, places, culture, and the world because of Jesus and his salvation—the "fount of every blessing." If you find *grace* in the Bible—anywhere—then you have encountered the active presence of Jesus and his salvation. Therefore, look at every discovered aspect of grace in the Bible not only as a rare thing, but also through a *gospel lens*. In other words, it is there only because of Jesus and his salvation. Period. In this way, every graced person, place, relationship, word, idea, image, story, history, action, event, institution, wisdom saying, and more in the Bible points to the *ultimate source or work of grace* in the Bible—Jesus and his salvation.

For example, 1 Samuel 27–31 is a story about two kings: Saul and David. The world of Saul is recorded first, then the world of David. Although recorded sequentially, both worlds occur simultaneously, heightening the comparison. In both accounts, Saul and David encounter a scary world that shakes them to the roots of their being. Interestingly, both are said to experience the same thing: unbearable weakness. Literally, Saul experiences "no strength in him" (28:20) and David experiences "no more strength" (30:4). In other words, they were both weak in themselves, unable in themselves, nothing in themselves. As are we. Yet something stunning separates the two in their weakness. David "strengthened himself in the Lord his God" (30:6); Saul did not. Saul "falls full length on the ground filled with fear" (28:20). Therefore, Saul sinks into the corpse of self and David rises in the strength of Another.[9]

What is happening here? *Grace* is happening here. The Apostle Paul would interpret what happens to David with the same words Jesus spoke to him in his own acute experience of weakness, "My grace is sufficient for you, for my power is made perfect in weakness" (2 Cor 12:9). The ultimate source and work of grace experienced by David in 1 Samuel 30 is Jesus and his salvation, that is, the ultimate strength of God. Perhaps it was the strength of God loving him amidst unbearable loss and severe rejection that strengthened David. Therefore, a *gospel lens* sees the ultimate source or work of grace revealed in the text to be the love of God in Jesus' loss and rejection. Perhaps it was the strength of God's stubborn habit to raise the dead (see the previous footnote), strengthen the weak, or perform twelfth-hour deliverances that strengthened David. Therefore, a *gospel lens* sees the ultimate source or work of grace revealed in the text to be Jesus' resurrection as the present strength to face any mini-death in life.

In sum, Pole 2 reads backwards or looks through a *gospel lens* to re-read or re-interpret the text to see more. Pole 2 is the second component of the Gospel Arc preaching model, the ultimate revelation of Jesus Christ and his salvation. Jesus Christ and his salvation changes everything, including how to read the Bible. A biblical text has not been accurately understood,

---

9. When did David rise from the death of Ziklag? The text literally says, "on the third day" (1 Samuel 30:1). The rest of 1 Samuel 30 pretty much documents David's victorious rise from the dead and the taking of a new Israel with him! Interestingly, the Apostle Paul records, "he (Jesus) was raised on the third day in accordance with the Scriptures" (1 Corinthians 15:4). What scriptures? The Old Testament scriptures. But no Old Testament scripture specifically mentions Jesus rising from the dead. Therefore, Paul must understand that resurrection from the dead lives deep in the bones of the Old Testament. In other words, it is a gospel thread.

applied, or communicated until it has been integrated with the overall gospel message of the Bible, Jesus Christ, and his salvation. Therefore, we must read backwards or re-read every text through the lens of the gospel. In this way, we see more.

Connect the Gospel Arc

Reading forward or following a *gospel thread* and reading backwards or looking through a *gospel lens*, work together to discover the *Textual Jesus* in the text. Learn to do both simultaneously, that is, learn to connect Pole 1 and Pole 2 to form a *Gospel Arc*.

The *Gospel Arc* connects Pole 1 (the text) to Pole 2 (the ultimate context) by reading forward from the text (Pole 1) to Jesus Christ and his salvation (Pole 2). In this way, Pole 1 provides a pattern of significance to Jesus Christ and his salvation from the text with which to work. Follow these *gospel threads* to Jesus and his salvation.

Simultaneously, the *Gospel Arc* connects Pole 2 (the ultimate context) to Pole 1 (the text) by reading backwards from Jesus Christ and his salvation (Pole 2) to the text (Pole 1). In this way, Pole 2 re-reads, re-interprets, completes, or maps more meaning inherent within the text so that more is seen. Look through the *gospel lens* of Jesus and his salvation to see the surplus of meaning hidden in the text revealed.

The goal of connecting this *Gospel Arc* is to discover a specific aspect of Jesus and his salvation in the text. In other words, the goal is a *Textual Jesus*. Once the *Gospel Arc* has been connected between Pole 1 and Pole 2, the preacher can now craft a specific *Textual Jesus* from the text into a sticky statement or vivid image. The sermon then is built around this *Textual Jesus* to reach and renew lives, homes, relationships, places, communities, and the surrounding culture.

For example, Song of Songs 3:1–5 is about love at night or love hurts, something that everyone knows from experience. But amazingly, Song of Songs 3.5 says *love* actually tells us this! Therefore, a human condition in the text could be: "'Love Hurts' says love." Love goes on to explain why it hurts—because our *soul* is involved (v. 2). And then love provides some practical help because it does hurt—work hard at love within the meaning of marriage (vv. 1–2, 4–5). Therefore, the Big Idea of the text could be: "'Love Hurts' says love." Ultimately, however, the woman does not find her lover because of her hard work (v. 3–4a); rather, he just shows up out of nowhere. It is a mystery, but in Wisdom literature, mystery is mostly where

God is! Mystery is where God shows up; therefore, love finally solves the mystery of love, "Love is ultimately found because of God."

Certainly, more can be said about the mystery of love in Song of Songs 3:1–5. To discover the *Textual Jesus*, however, follow the *gospel thread* of "love is ultimately found because of God" to Jesus and his salvation. Simultaneously, look through a *gospel lens* at the text to see more (reread). Perhaps, the more you see is the lost lover (the man) in the text. And you see love go out at night to find the lost and will not stop until it does. In other words, you see how love will sacrificially love and love and love . . . the lost. How do we know love loves like this? "Just ask Jesus," love says. This could be a *Textual Jesus* from Song of Songs 3:1–5 as you connect Pole 1 to Pole 2.

Craft a Textual Jesus

At this point in the Gospel Arc preaching model, Pole 1 and Pole 2 have been connected. The original historical meaning of the text has been interpreted and recorded into three sticky statements or vivid images concerning: 1) a specific aspect of the universal human condition being addressed in the text, 2) the primary thing the text is saying (the text's Big Idea), and 3) the primary thing the text is doing with what it is saying (the text's Applied Big Idea). A connection has been made between the original historical meaning of the text and Jesus Christ and his salvation or the ultimate meaning of the text. The connection was made by reading forward from the text to Jesus Christ and his salvation and by reading backwards from Jesus Christ and his salvation to the text.

In sum, the two poles of the Gospel Arc preaching model have been connected. It is time to craft a specific *Textual Jesus* from the text.

How do you craft a specific *Textual Jesus* from the text? The answer is to think of Pole 1 and Pole 2 as two lumps of clay that need to be crafted into the Jesus of the text. Practically, this means taking the two lumps of clay (Pole 1 and Pole 2) and crafting one specific aspect of Jesus Christ and his salvation from the text into either a sticky statement or vivid image.

The freshly crafted *Textual Jesus* is the specific aspect of Jesus Christ and his salvation revealed in the text to reach and renew lives. The sermon now is built around this freshly crafted *Textual Jesus*.

For example, in Song of Songs 3:1–5, the *gospel thread* was "love is ultimately found because of God" (Pole 1). When looking through the *gospel lens* at the text to re-read it, the more that is seen is the "lost lover" (the Pole 2). Connect the poles or form a *Gospel Arc*. Or take the two lumps of clay and craft a *Textual Jesus*. Therefore, the crafting process (mental process) could look something like: 1) love goes out at night to find the lost and will not stop until it does, 2) How do we know love does this? 3) the answer is the *Textual Jesus*: "'Just ask Jesus,' love says."

AN EXAMPLE FROM ROMANS 10:1-4

1. *Read Forward*. When I read forward from Pole 1 (the text) to Jesus and his salvation (Pole 2), "the righteousness from God" becomes my gospel thread.
2. *Read Backwards*. When I read backwards from Pole 2 (Jesus and his salvation) to the text (Pole 1), my gospel lens sees Jesus' achieved righteousness as the righteousness from God.
3. Craft a specific *Textual Jesus* from the text. When I connect the Poles (Pole 1 and Pole 2), "Jesus is all the righteousness you need" hits my head and heart.
4. The Textual Jesus: Jesus is all the righteousness you need.

Chapter 9

Craft a Sermon Message

Once the text's original historical message (Pole 1) and the ultimate message of Jesus Christ and his salvation (Pole 2) have been connected or arced to form a *Textual Jesus* (either as a sticky statement or vivid image), it is time to craft a sermon message and build a sermon map.

The sermon message is the one powerful thing you are saying from the text. The sermon map is how you communicate the one powerful thing to your hearers. In other words, once you have crafted a sermon message, build everything around it. And finally, speak others back to life again.

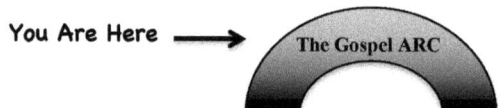

*Build the Sermon Around the *Textual Jesus*
**A Gospel ARC Sermon is Built Around Re-Presenting Jesus Christ & His Salvation according to the Particular Way of the Text in a Way that is Clear to the Mind and Real to the Heart

The Gospel Arc

ROUND 5: CRAFT THE SERMON MESSAGE

1. The sermon should say and do one *powerful thing* not many things. Therefore, craft a *Sermon Message*. Pick a point!

Sermon Message Tool 1.

First, a Sermon Message is crafted around the five interpretive tracks below:

1. Your recorded sticky statement or vivid image for the *universal human* and/or *cultural condition* being specifically addressed in the text.
2. Your recorded sticky statement or vivid image for the text's *Big Idea* (or the primary thing the passage is saying).
3. Your recorded sticky statement or vivid image for the text's *Applied Big Idea* (or the primary thing the passage is doing with what it is saying).
4. Your recorded sticky statement or vivid image for the *Textual Jesus* (or the specific aspect of Jesus Christ and his salvation revealed in the text).
5. The specific human and/or cultural need of *contemporary hearers* (the local listening need).

Sermon Message Tool 2

Second, there are three preferred ways to craft a Sermon Message around the five interpretive tracks above.

1. *Blend them all together* into one *sticky statement, vivid image,* or *suspenseful question*. Whether blended together into one sticky statement, vivid image, or suspenseful question, the individual tracks become the supporting ideas or movements of the Sermon Map.

   Sticky Statement:
   Vivid Image:
   Or Suspenseful Question:

2. *Lead with one track while the other tracks stand off stage* waiting to make key appearances during the event of the sermon. In other words, the lead track rules them all by becoming the Sermon Message and the other tracks play key supporting roles as needed in the Sermon Map.

   Lead Track:
   Supporting Track(s):

3. *Follow a narrative form* that places the individual tracks into the plot line of one ultimate over-arching story or Sermon Message. In other words, "This is a story about ___." What you fill in is your Sermon Message. How you tell the story is your Sermon Map.

This is a story about _____." This is your Sermon Message:
Tell the story with the individual Interpretive Tracks (Sermon Map):

2. Once you have *Crafted a Sermon Message*, build everything around it. Build a *Sermon Map* in oral form (natural scripting to be heard not read). Keep in mind:

- The aim of preaching is to experience Jesus Christ and his salvation with the text in order to reach and renew lives, the home, relationships, the church, places, communities, and the surrounding culture.
- In other words, the aim of preaching is gospel-growth in people.
- Therefore, the *Sermon Map* should best support this aim.

A Gospel Arc sermon is built around a *Textual Jesus*, that is, a specific aspect of Jesus and his salvation revealed in the text. This is done in a way that is both clear to the mind and real to the heart. Crafting a Gospel Arc sermon is the fifth round of the Gospel Arc preaching model and involves three major movements: 1) crafting the sermon message, 2) building a sermon map in oral form, and 3) speaking others back to life again.

INSTRUCTION

Craft a Sermon Message

The sermon should say and do one powerful thing, not many things. Therefore, pick a point! Certainly, there are supporting ideas and running applications throughout the sermon. These, however, should support one powerful sermon message, not pull in several directions at once.

How does one craft a single powerful sermon message? There are many ways to do this, as the growing library of preaching books demonstrate. The Gospel Arc preaching model approaches crafting a sermon message around five interpretive textual tracks that mutually inform each other:

1. The recorded sticky statement or vivid image for the *universal human condition* being specifically addressed in the text.

2. The recorded sticky statement or vivid image for the text's *Big Idea* or the primary thing the passage is saying.

3. The recorded sticky statement or vivid image for the text's *Applied Big Idea* or the primary thing the passage is doing with what it is saying.

4. The recorded sticky statement or vivid image for the *Textual Jesus* or the specific aspect of Jesus Christ and his salvation revealed in the text.

5. The new consideration of the specific human and/or cultural needs of one's hearers or the local listening need.

These four textual interpretive tracks plus the new local listening track must converge or blend into one sermon message. The Gospel Arc preaching model prefers three approaches to accomplish this:

1. Blend them all together into one sticky statement, vivid image, or suspenseful question to craft the sermon message. Whether blended together into one sticky statement, vivid image, or suspenseful question, the individual tracks then become the key supporting ideas or movements of the Sermon Map.

2. Lead with one track while the other tracks stand off stage waiting to make key appearances during the event of the sermon. In other words, the lead track rules them all by becoming the Sermon Message while the other tracks play key supporting roles as needed in the Sermon Map.

3. Follow a narrative form that places the individual tracks into the plot line of one ultimate over-arching story or Sermon Message. In other words, "This is a story about _____." What you fill in is your Sermon Message. How you tell the story is your Sermon Map.

Practically speaking, exegesis can go on forever. There is always more to learn and one more commentary to read. It is time to STOP. It is time to walk among the bones of your work until God brings them to life! That is, until the Holy Spirit gives you a Sermon Message.

The walk among the bones of your work looking for a Sermon Message to arise looks like listening to your five interpretive tracks of the text, mentally chewing on them, talking to God about them, sifting through them collectively, thinking about them in a relaxed way while doing something else (walking, working out, driving, day dreaming, reading, enjoying an adult beverage, and so on), and ultimately picking a point where the sermon is going. In this way, a Sermon Message resurrects from the bones of your work. Raised by the power of the Holy Spirit, of course.

Take for example, Hebrews 12:1–2. Perhaps your interpretive tracks look something like: 1) the struggle of the Christian life (human condition), 2) the Christian life is running a race (Big Idea), 3) run and run and run (Applied Big Idea), 4) there is only One Runner in all human history to cross the finish line (Textual Jesus), and 5) the need to run by faith instead of effort (local listening need).

If these five interpretive tracks are blended together, the Sermon Message could be a suspenseful question: "What does the Christian life look like, really?" Then you arrange the five interpretive tracks to answer and/or develop the question. How you answer and/or develop the question is the Sermon Map.

If "run and run and run" (the Applied Big Idea) becomes the one track that rules them all, then it is the Sermon Message. The other four tracks play key supporting roles as needed to best develop "run and run and run" in the Sermon Map.

Or, if this is a story about the struggle of the Christian life, then the human condition is the Sermon Message. Now, tell the story with the remaining interpretive tracks. How you tell the story is your Sermon Map.

Build a Sermon Map

Once the Sermon Message has been crafted, build everything around it. This is your Sermon Map. A Sermon Map answers, "How does the Sermon Message speak others back to life again?" or "How can my listeners best hear the Sermon Message?" or "How do I unleash the Sermon Message upon my hearers?" or "How do I launch the Sermon Message to reach and renew lives and the world?" The aim of preaching is to experience Jesus and his salvation with the Bible by faith. It is to experience the *Textual Jesus* who reaches and renews lives, the home, relationships, the church, places, communities, the surrounding culture, and the world. In other words, the aim of preaching is gospel-growth in people everywhere (Col 1).

Therefore, the Sermon Map should best support the aim of experiencing Jesus and his salvation with the text by faith or gospel growth in people. It should map out the Sermon Message in a way that encounters the *Textual Jesus*.

Generally, all sermon maps include some form of introduction, body, and conclusion. Specifically, the text's own literary form can supply a Sermon Map. Also, many preaching resources provide helpful sermon map ideas that can be creatively cannibalized for your own mapping purposes.

The Gospel Arc Preaching model, however, employs three broad sermon maps to help you get started.

The first Sermon Map is *Blend Everything*. Once you have blended all five of your interpretive tracks together into one sticky statement, vivid image, or suspenseful question to craft the sermon message, build a Sermon Map with the materials already in your possession—your five interpretive tracks. Simply arrange your five interpretive tracks to best deliver the Sermon Message in an engaging way. A Sermon Map arranged to maintain tension is always effective. Therefore, hook them and then keep them glued to the text. Jesus is the master maintainer of tension.

For example, if your blended Sermon Message is a suspenseful question, then build a Sermon Map that ultimately answers the suspenseful question. How? By unpacking the five interpretive tracks piece by suspenseful piece. Therefore, *Blend Everything* to discover your Sermon Message, and then *Blend Everything* into the key supporting ideas or movements of the Sermon Map in a suspenseful way.

The second Sermon Map is *Pick One Track to Rule Them All*. Once you have picked one of your five interpretive tracks to rule them all for your Sermon Message, build a Sermon Map with the remaining four interpretive tracks. In other words, lead with one track (Sermon Message) while the other four tracks stand off stage waiting to make key appearances throughout the divine drama of the sermon (the Sermon Map).

For example, if your Sermon Message is the Big Idea in the text (either in the form of a suspenseful question, sticky statement, or vivid image) then build a Sermon Map with the remaining Human Condition, Applied Big Idea, Textual Jesus, and Local Listening Need. Therefore, pick one track to rule them all (Sermon Message), and then marshal the remaining four tracks to play key supporting roles as needed in the Sermon Map.

The third sermon map is *Tell the Story*. Once you have discovered your Sermon Message by supplying the answer to, "This is a story about ___," build a Sermon Map that tells the story. Identify the story (Sermon Message), then tell the story with your interpretive tracks (Sermon Map).

For example, if your sermon message is a story about an aspect of the human condition in the text, then build a sermon map that best tells that story. Employ the Big Idea, Applied Big Idea, Textual Jesus, and the Local Listening Need to tell the story.

One more thought about your Sermon Map. The sermon is not a literary product to be read but an oral message to be heard and experienced. Therefore, whatever Sermon Map you employ, follow an oral form rather than a literary one. In other words, natural scripting should always prevail over whatever form your sermon notes take—even over what your English teacher taught you.

Speak Others Back to Life Again

Preaching is a divine event in which the preacher participates. In other words, God speaks people back to life again in preaching, including the preacher. Therefore, both the preacher and hearer should dress appropriately—with crash helmets and seat belts. The aim of preaching for both the preacher and the hearer is to experience Jesus and his salvation with the text by faith, resulting in change-on-the-spot or gospel growth. For the preacher, gospel growth begins with preparation and continues with proclamation—or by experiencing the text in preparation and then re-experiencing the text in proclamation.

Understanding preaching as a divine event in which Jesus shows up with his comprehensive salvation to reach and renew lives, relationships, places, and the world not only energizes your preparation and proclamation but also sets you free from the multiform prisons of self. You are free to expect God to work in your sermon preparation and proclamation. You are free to be a part of what God is already doing in your sermon preparation and proclamation. Therefore, the burden of trying to make something happen, that is, to activate God and his work in your life, ministry, and the world has been cast upon Another.

You are free. Free to be a nothing, while Jesus is everything. Free to simply be a part of what God is already doing. Free to be yourself (natural), forget yourself, and be absorbed in preaching, which is, your best and most effective preaching style.[1] Free to speak others back to life again, as God works in you and through you. Taking Jesus with you in preaching changes everything.

AN EXAMPLE FROM ROMANS 10:1-4[2]

Craft a Sermon Message

Gather the work of my four interpretive tracks for Romans 10:1-4:

1. The *Human Condition*: The deep struggle for righteousness.
2. The *Big Idea*: The end of the deep struggle for righteousness.

---

1. Lloyd-Jones, *Preaching and Preachers*, 264.
2. See Appendix III for the complete sermon transcript of Romans 10:1-4.

3. The *Applied Big Idea*: End your deep struggle for righteousness and help others do the same.
4. The *Textual Jesus*: Jesus is all the righteousness you need.

Now add the *Local Listening Need*. The universal experience of chaos during the 2020 Pandemic easily becomes the local listening need.

When I walk among the bones of the five interpretive tracks above with God (i.e., prayerful thinking in the presence of God), the *Local Listening Need* becomes the one that rules them all. Therefore, it becomes the *Sermon Message*.

The *Sermon Message* (i.e., the Local Listening Need) is put in the form of a suspenseful question: What do we do when we're all crazy?

The answer(s) to the *Sermon Message* become the *Sermon Map*. Note that the answer(s) will come from your other four interpretive tracks.

Build a *Sermon Map*

The answer(s) to the *Sermon Message* become your *Sermon Map*. Take note that your supplied answer(s) will come from the work you've already done with your four interpretive tracks.

Sermon Message:
What do we do when we're all crazy?
Sermon Map:
Don't be stupid about what's going on.
End your struggle for righteousness, and help others do the same.

Build a *Sermon Map* in an *Oral Script*

This is to be heard, not read, according to the *Sermon's Movement*. Make your sermon move. Start with your notes!

For example, my sermon notes are arranged according to Movement 1, Movement 2, Movement 3, etc. . . headings at the top of each page. Thinking, preparing, and preaching in terms of movement pushes preaching in a dynamic direction (preaching as divine event), as opposed to a stagnant direction (preaching as lecture). Therefore, my *Sermon Map* moves this way:

> Movement 1: Zeal without knowledge (truth, reality) is everywhere
>   Funny story
>   Scary examples
>   Connect to Romans 10:1–4

>   What do we do when we're all crazy?
>   Read Romans 10:1–4
>   Pray
>
>   Movement 2: Don't be stupid about what's going on
>   What do we do when we're all crazy?
>   First, don't be stupid about what's going on (v. 3)
>   There's a deeper struggle going on
>   What's the deeper struggle?
>   The deeper struggle for righteousness
>   Illustrate
>   Apply
>
>   Movement 3: End your struggle for righteousness
>   What do we do when we're all crazy?
>   Second, end your struggle for righteousness (v. 4)
>   Jesus ends the deep struggle for righteousness
>   How? By giving you HIS
>   "the righteousness from God"
>   "from God"
>   There is no righteousness "from us"
>   Illustrate
>   Apply
>   A Jesus-righteousness is the only power that can end your struggle for righteousness
>   Jesus is all the righteousness you need
>   Illustrate
>   Apply
>
>   Movement 4: Help others end the deeper struggle
>   The struggle for righteousness is over
>   Jesus is all the righteousness you need
>   You are free to help others end their struggle

CONCLUSIONS

There you have it, the five rounds of The Gospel Arc Preaching Manual: 1) Listen to the Text, 2) Understand the Text, 3) Discover the Text's Message, 4) Discover the Textual Jesus, and 5) Craft a Sermon Message. It is designed to give some concrete help and direction toward taking Jesus with you in preaching. It is the product of help and direction that has come to me over the years from a mixture of personal experience and a multiplicity of sources that can no longer be distinguished and separated from my own experience. In other words, their help to me runs that deep.³ It also is an eternally unfinished Frankenstein-like creation. Significant pieces and parts still await assembly. My hope is that the Gospel Arc Preaching Model adds some significant pieces and parts to your call to speak people back to life again.

Like you I crave the concrete. Therefore, I would be tempted to close the book at this point. However, keep reading! Don't stop! What awaits you in the remaining chapters is the biblical-theological power that informs, forms, and energizes each individual round of the Gospel Arc Preaching Model. What awaits you is perhaps further spiritual formation and ministry around the Gospel. What awaits you is perhaps the experience of deeper energies at work in the world. What awaits you is the challenge to take Jesus with you not only in preaching but also all of life, thereby, changing everything.

---

3. It is safe to say that anyone in the acknowledgments, endorsements, and Bibliography are to be credited with profoundly shaping my understanding and practice of taking Jesus with you in preaching.

PART 4

The Biblical-Theological Power of the Gospel Arc

Chapter 10

The Power of Listening to the Text

BE AN INTELLIGENT MYSTIC

Intelligent mysticism is experiencing Jesus and his salvation (mysticism) with the Bible (intelligent), not apart from it. Today and throughout church history, we tend to fall into one of two camps.[1] Camp one is the "intelligent camp." These are the truth experts. Knowing God in this camp is about objective truth, theology, doctrine, propositions, getting it right, the life of the mind, and truth-telling. Camp two is the "mystical camp." These are the experience experts. Knowing God in this camp is about spiritual experience, the inner life, contemplative spirituality, spiritual disciplines, communion with God, getting it felt, the life of the heart, and feeling deeply.

These two camps embody church traditions, denominations, and movements throughout church history. These two camps tend to be suspicious of each other, and interestingly seem to divide nicely along personality tendencies as well.

The danger of separating *experience* from truth for the Christian is real. Truth does not float above experience in a weird realm called "abstraction." Truth is not biblical information to be downloaded or biblical principles to be mechanically memorized, mastered, and applied. Truth is living and

---

1. Keller and Clowney, "Preaching Christ in a Postmodern World."

active, ultimately a Person and his comprehensive work in all its activating and energizing implications.

Therefore, truth not only *says* something but also *does* something. The truth is God creates me, loves me, redeems me, wins me, forgives me, justifies me, sanctifies me, shepherds me, calls me, enlightens me, protects and defends me, unites me to his body the church and its mission, uses me as an instrument in his hands, and will raise me from the dead at the end of all things. Truth is inherently personal, relational, experiential, dynamic, or transformative because it is reality (meaning) itself. It is impossible for truth to be abstract.

Furthermore, the deeply dynamic nature of truth includes its legal wonders. For example, some seem to approach the legal reality of justification in a shockingly sterile way, which certainly explains its lack of spiritual electricity in some places. Others simply discard it as a legal fiction or strangely allow their ecclesiology to swallow it up, thereby making it irrelevant.

No matter how hard we try, however, the need to be justified is not going away. It is a universal human condition. We come into this world with a justification-shaped and justification-sized hole in the soul needing to be filled (Gen 3). Therefore, the good news that the struggle for righteousness is over (legally) is simultaneously deeply personal, experiential, dynamic, and dare I say sanctifying for the Christian.

What can reach and renew the roots of one's being more than God ending the impossible struggle for righteousness with the grace of his Son's own righteousness? What can be more freeing and healing than freedom from the oppressive force of condemnation (legal power) that universally breaks down lives, relationships, and places everywhere (dynamic power)? What creates a more intact identity before God, oneself, others, and all of life than a received-righteousness from God himself? What changes a life more than the justifying love of Jesus personally and actively present in his incarnation, life, death, resurrection, and present reign? In other words, justification changes everything!

Furthermore, justification is a legal power that carries dynamic power with it. "Justification is not the goal but the source of love and service . . . Paul moves from 'no condemnation' to 'new creation' in a logical sequence of sentences"[2] in Romans 8:1–4. In other words, justification (legal source) carries dynamic life or the Holy Spirit with it just as condemnation (legal source) carries dynamic death with it (vv. 1–2).

---

2. Horton, *Justification*, 365.

Even human relationships bear this out practically. Welcoming, accepting, affirming, and praising others carries life with it. Being "justified" by another loves you back to life again! Accusing, judging, rejecting, and condemning someone carries death with it. Being "condemned" by another breaks down a life.

In this way, justification is the legal source for the dynamic power of the "Spirit of life" (vv. 1–2). Negatively speaking, sin or the "Adamic-self" is put to death on the cross legally (no more condemnation), and therefore also dynamically (no more bondage), as "our old self was crucified with him in order that the body of Sin might be brought to nothing" (Rom 6:6).

Positively speaking, when Jesus exited the tomb, he took us with him. In Romans 5:18, Paul says Jesus' resurrection is the Christian's justification (legal power) and life (dynamic power). In other words, a "new-self" emerged with Jesus from the tomb that is not only righteous legally (justification), but additionally alive with the gift of a new dynamic nature by the Spirit.[3]

Therefore, it is absolutely impossible for the truth of justification to be abstract, impersonal, or inactive in one's life. It is impossible for it to be a legal fiction in any meaningful way. It is a truth that sets you free to finally be yourself, forget yourself, and live outside yourself in faith toward God and with love and service toward others. In justification, we are finally human again. We are free to exercise dominion by loving and serving the world back to life again with our time, talents, and work without the fear of looking over our shoulder for the hostile powers of condemnation (1 John 4:18) or using others and creation for our own self-saving ends. Sanctification is a justified life in action.

The danger of separating *truth* from experience for the Christian is also real. Jesus and his salvation is not an experience *apart from truth*. It is experiencing Truth, that is, the revelatory person and work of redemption.

Generally speaking, all human beings as image-bearers experience God's revelatory work of creation regardless the level of awareness and suppression (Ps 19; Rom 1:18–32). Simultaneously, all human beings, as fallen image-bearers, also experience the futility of creation due to sin (Rom 8:18–21), again regardless the level of awareness and suppression.

The Bible describes the experience of creation (general truth) and redemption (special truth) by faith as wisdom and human flourishing. It describes the alternate experience of sin and death (the lies of de-creation) by unbelief as human foolishness and misery. Therefore, the experience of

---

3. The new creation is typically differentiated as definitive sanctification leading to progressive sanctification, and ultimately to glorification.

the truth of redemption by faith is dynamically life-giving. It results in gratitude, worship, awe, love, humility, repentance, life change, good works, and wisdom; in other words, sanctification.

In Jesus' high priestly prayer in John 17:3 he says, "And this is eternal life, that they may know you the only true God, and Jesus Christ whom you have sent." According to Jesus, both camps are right. To "know" in John 17:3 means both clarity in the mind and realness in the heart, both light in one's understanding and heat in one's experience, both truth in thought and life in emotion.

Knowing God is experiencing truth. It is the inscripturated truth of Jesus and his salvation in the Bible passing into the soul. It is the Word become flesh speaking us back to life again—in, through, and with the inscripturated-Word.

Therefore, knowing God is both intelligent and mystical. Choosing between truth and experience is a false choice. It is always both/and, not either/or. To know God, we must become an intelligent mystic. Jesus is praying we become one (John 17).

LEARN THE MYSTERY OF LIFE CHANGE

Many approaches to life change leave Jesus behind. Approaches to life change, renewal, or sanctification seem to cluster around three global views. Perhaps you can relate to one or more, or all three: 1) Antinomian life change, 2) Moralistic life change, and 3) Gospel life change.

Antinomian Life Change

Antinomian life change does not believe in life change, either formally or functionally. It is anti-law or relativistic in its approach to life and ministry. Therefore, it avoids God and the spiritual fabric (moral law) of the universe by self-creating its own world and laws out of nothing.

In this way, antinomian life change attempts to generate its own truth, righteousness, identity, meaning, happiness, freedom, flourishing, humanness, the good life, or salvation. It seeks to save itself through lawless or irreligious strategies that ironically are a form of laws or works. It leaves Jesus behind. Jesus diagnoses the antinomian biography in the story of the lost younger son in Luke 15.[4] Christians generally avoid this approach to life change, well, at least in formal belief.

---

4. See Keller's, *Prodigal God,* for a masterful and life-changing exposition of the

Moralistic Life Change

Moralism believes in life-change, but it is the self-activating kind. The most common form is self-activating life change driven by human will or some form of law keeping. Jesus diagnoses the moralist's biography in the story of the lost older son in Luke 15. Moralism, historically speaking, is Pelagianism, which most Christians try to avoid.

A hidden form of moralism exists, however, that is harder to detect. It is also the self-activating kind, but in the spiritual context of activating God and/or the Holy Spirit in one's life. It is life-change by a mixture of Jesus (or some notion of grace on a spectrum) *plus* something. It is faith *plus* some form of human effort or law principle. It is a causal-cooperation between God and the Christian for life-change.

Think of a big ole' pot of stew (I'm from Texas) with the gospel (grace) and the law (human effort) thrown in. The mixture makes something new (i.e., neo-nomism or a "new law"). The new stew is semi-Pelagian life-change. It has come in a variety of forms throughout church history, but its core is the same: Jesus *plus* something, faith *plus* something, or a weird mixture of law and gospel that is neither law nor gospel. Later, I refer to this strange cocktail as a "third word" from God beyond God's two words of law and gospel. At best, it is an impotent human concoction; at worst, it is our active enemy at work corrupting our faith.

In semi-Pelagian life change, "the law and the flesh commends life" in cooperation with God.[5] Therefore, sanctification ultimately functions "by works of the law" rather than "by hearing with faith," which is precisely what Paul is arguing against in Galatians 3:1–6. Semi-Pelagian life change is ultimately a form of self-sanctification, which inherently undermines a Jesus-justification. This was Paul's great concern for the Galatians.

Whether moralism is the Pelagian or semi-Pelagian variety, it seeks to be its own lord and savior. It leaves Jesus behind. It self-activates sanctification or the Holy Spirit in the Christian for sanctification. Instead of employing a lawless strategy like antinomian life change, however, it employs a lawful one. Walter Marshall says moralistic life change is exactly what cannot change a life:

> You cannot be sanctified by your own endeavors. You cannot produce holiness in yourself. You can only attain holiness by faith in Christ's death and resurrection—the very same faith

---

story of the world, that is, the story of the daughters and sons of Adam and Eve communicated in the two lost sons of Luke 15.

5. Luther, *Commentary on Galatians*, 137.

that justifies you. The law only stirs up sin in you. You must be freed from the law if you are going to attain any holiness at all, as the Apostle Paul teaches—Romans 6:11–14, 7:1–6. This way of sanctification by faith confirms the doctrine of justification by faith, as Paul says—Romans 8.1.[6]

Therefore, any approach to sanctification *not* driven by faith alone in Jesus and his salvation, leaves Jesus behind.

Furthermore, moralistic life change builds a model for life change upon a faulty view of the Christian. It views the Christian as a continuous spiritual-self who simply needs some activating help. The activating help can come from an endless supply of options depending upon the tradition, theology, or special anointed individual.

The Christian, however, is not a continuous spiritual-self on a victory march. She is a conflicted-self in a spiritual battle. She possess a radical duality or split-ness. The Christian is a mixture of two natures, flesh and spirit (Rom 6–8, Gal 5, Eph 4–6).

It could be said that the Christian is simultaneously justified and sinful, loved and evil, accepted as righteous and curved in on themselves, an old self and a new self. The Christian life is a civil war between two selves—the old self in Adam, and the new self in Christ. It is a real battle, not the Pixar kind. The losses and pain are real. Ultimately, however, because of Jesus, it is a battle that cannot be lost.

Therefore, any meaningful approach to life change must address the Christian as a conflicted-self. Biblical renewal, life change, or sanctification must involve the divine activity of the two words of God, that is, law and gospel. The law addresses the hidden "old self" (aka, the flesh, sinful nature, body of death, Adamic-self, collapsed self, shadow self, false self) in need of being "put off" (Eph 4:22). The gospel addresses the "new self" in need of being "put on" by faith in Jesus and his salvation.

The "putting off" and "putting on," however, are not self-activating but rather what faith simply does as it experientially trusts in Jesus and what he has already done (i.e., Paul's "hearing of faith" in Galatians 3:1–7). It is believing the gospel in real time. It is functionally putting off the old-self and putting on the new-self in specific areas of life or struggle by faith in the life, death, and resurrection of Jesus. It is taking the gospel to the unevangelized areas of our lives and relationships. It is walking by faith. It is walking in the Spirit.

Biblical life change is not achieving higher levels of holiness but simply being who you already are in Christ—functionally, experientially, by faith.

---

6. Marshall, *Gospel Mystery of Sanctification*, 231.

The Apostle Paul summarizes renewal, life change, or sanctification as a gospel life: "I have been crucified with Christ. I live but no longer I, but Christ lives in me. And the life I now live in the flesh I live by faith in the Son of God who loved me and gave himself for me" (Gal 2:20, my translation).

Being "filled with the Holy Spirit" (Eph 5:18) is being filled with the gospel of Jesus and his salvation by faith in real life and messy relationships. Walking around in the Spirit is walking around in the good news of Jesus and his salvation in all life by faith (Gal 5). The Christian life is learning to build your messy life, relationships, work, good works, obedience, ministry, various gifts, and specific aspects of life (like how you handle money) around Jesus and his salvation. It is a gospel life.

The Christian as a conflicted-self in a spiritual battle (Eph 6) is in direct conflict with the notion of the Christian being a continuous spiritual-self on a victory march. The continuous spiritual-self gets in the way of the Holy Spirit's ordinary work in a life and community. It produces anxiety due to the inability to control or manage the victory march. It enslaves in a psychological prison; a swinging back and forth between spiritual mania (when measuring up) and spiritual depression (when falling short). Ironically, the basis for each spiritual mood swing is fundamentally static: one's performance. Tragically, Jesus' performance, though perhaps intellectually affirmed, is experientially absent in any meaningful or sanctifying way.

Therefore, the continuous spiritual-self is delusional because it avoids any meaningful engagement with the "old self" still attached to or active in the Christian. And it is destructive because it avoids any meaningful engagement with Jesus and his salvation experientially in the Christian life. In the end, the Christian life is reduced to trying to activate God in your life. There is a need for preaching that experiences Jesus with the Bible by faith for sanctification, renewal, or life change.

Gospel Life Change

Gospel life change believes in life change, but unlike moralistic life change, it believes in life change by the power of the gospel alone. It is life change by faith in Jesus and his salvation alone. It is life change by the gospel's energies and activation alone, and not some form of self-activation (even if it is with God's help). If life change is swimming, then the pool is the gospel. Therefore, sanctification, like justification, is by grace alone through faith alone on account of Christ alone, period. This kind of sanctification is the Spirit-filled life.

Gospel life change relies upon the power of the gospel, union with Christ, or Jesus and his salvation to change or renew lives. It relies upon the finished and comprehensive work of Jesus and his salvation to change lives and relationships. It relies upon the divine life and saving power inherent in and released by the message of the gospel to sanctify lives and relationships (Rom 1:16, 1 Pet, and Col 1:5–7). It rests upon the person and work of Jesus Christ by his Spirit not only to justify the collapsed-self of the ungodly *but also* to sanctify the conflicted-self of the godly.

Gospel life change rejoices and boasts in no other work outside the gospel for both justification and sanctification. In other words, Jesus and his salvation is enough to justify and to sanctify a life—no other work is needed. In this way, sanctification by faith in Jesus and his salvation changes lives, relationships, and communities.

The Apostle Paul links being ashamed of the gospel to any form of Jesus *plus* something (human effort, work, or law principle), "For I am not ashamed of the gospel, for it is the power of God for salvation to everyone who *believes*" (Rom 1:16). The gospel is the power of God for a comprehensive salvation—justification, sanctification, and glorification—to everyone who *believes*, that is, trusts in Jesus and his salvation alone. The rest of the book of Romans unpacks the wonders of Jesus' comprehensive salvation. Each page unleashes divine energies to reach and renew the world on-the-spot. According to Paul, the failure to embrace gospel life change is an embodiment of being ashamed of the gospel (Rom 1:16). In this way, Paul anticipates a Pelagian and semi-Pelagian approach to justification *and* sanctification. He knew the universal human condition way before theological labels came along.

Is Gospel Life Change Antinomian?

Of course not! Antinomian life change does not believe in life change. Gospel life change believes in life change, that is, life change by the power of the gospel alone.

Therefore, "the gospel does not have an ounce of Antinomianism in it."[7] Luther says, gospel life change is typically slandered as antinomian by "unlearned idiots."[8] Moralistic life change simply cannot fathom a world where grace alone actually changes everything—individual lives, the home, relationships, pastors, the church, neighborhoods, communities, all kinds of places, the culture, and the world.

7. Marshall, *Gospel Mystery of Sanctification*, 22.
8. Luther, *Commentary on Galatians*, 43.

There is a fundamental inability in moralistic life change to see the unholy, hellish, and condemnable ways the heart pursues obedience and holiness (Gal 3:1–6). Both Jesus and the Apostle Paul spend significant amounts of time addressing the spiritually dead phenomenon of moralistic life change, and the utter futility of trying to perfect yourself *in* the flesh (Gal 3:3). The flesh cannot be figured out and fixed; it must be killed. It is important to realize that the failure to understand the dynamics of gospel life change do not make it untrue. Rather, it simply highlights its need and relevancy, as well as the power of original sin.

Is Gospel Life Change Inactivity?

No. The gospel reaches and renews people, not rocks. Therefore, gospel life change is always dynamic and active. As Paul says, "it [the gospel] is bearing fruit and increasing—as it also does among you, since the day you heard it and understood the grace of God in truth" (Col 1:6). The gospel grows in people, relationships, and places; it has an active course all of its own.

God works personally and actively through his gospel by his Spirit in messy people and relationships (Phil 2:12). Biblical life change is gospel growth in people (Col 1). It is a faith that comes by hearing (Rom 10) and that is active in love, good works, or in bearing fruit (Gal 5:6) as it remains in the Vine (John 15). In other words, biblical life change is work, activity, or swimming in the right place: the gospel. "This is the work of God, that you believe in him whom he sent"—Jesus (John 6:29).

Chapter 11

The Power of Understanding the Text

THE UN-CAGED LION

Lions are the "King of the Jungle." Awesome beauty. Raw, violent power. Lions must kill to live. One male lion will eat seventy-five pounds of meat in one meal. They can overpower and drag a six-hundred-pound Zebra. Have you ever heard a lion roar? Animal Planet does not count.

Several years ago, when our kids were spaced at nine, seven, five, three, and our fifth was a future "surprise" nine years away, we visited the Pittsburgh Zoo. It is one of the first natural habitat zoos, which meant moving more toward open habitations and away from cages.

It happened while we were walking toward Pride Rock to gawk at the lions. About a football field away, two lions started fighting, and they were not playing. When they roared, mothers instinctively clutched their children. Fathers scanned the walkway for a lion on the loose. Stomachs flipped. Knees buckled. Courage melted. The liturgy of terror was everywhere.

What if you were in a room full of people and I rolled a cage into the room, and in the cage was a lion. What if I reached over and lifted the latch to the cage, careful to place myself *behind* its steel opening. Stay with me, and what if the King of the Jungle walked out into the room with you? Who needs to be protected? The lion or *you*? The Bible is no ordinary book. It is an un-caged lion.

THE BIBLE DOES WHAT IT SAYS

"Let there be light" (Gen 1:3). God overcomes the darkness with verbal power at the beginning of all things. Imagine if light said, "Let me think about it!" During the great creative acts of God in Genesis, Scripture does not record God verbally expressing his wish and then acting wordlessly; rather, Scripture records God's speaking as his acting. The connection between God speaking and God acting is so enmeshed in the Scriptures that they are not only one and the same, but they are equated with God's presence: "The voice of the Lord breaks the cedars; the Lord breaks in pieces the cedars of Lebanon. . . . The voice of the Lord shakes the wilderness: the Lord shakes the wilderness of Kadesh (Ps 29:5, 8)."

Perhaps no one has said it better than Timothy Ward in his short book on the Scriptures, "as we encounter his words, and as we encounter the actions he performs by means of them, we are encountering God Himself." The nature of the Bible as divine "speech act"[1] presupposes that words do more than just "convey information, they get things done."[2] The Bible as divine speech act asserts not only that God's speaking and God's acting are one and the same, but also that God is personally and actively present in human lives and the world by his Scripture-Words.[3]

Timothy Ward asserts that non-speech act views of the Bible have one fundamental flaw—separating the Spirit's revelatory authority and active presence (or saving work) from the Scriptures. Therefore, Scripture is either replaced with the church (Catholic view), moral principles (conservative evangelical view), special anointed individuals (Charismatic view), or the human heart (Anabaptist view).[4]

Keller unites the Spirit and Scripture together in a God-ordained union. Therefore, the hearer of the Bible has personal access to God and his gracious work in their lives:

---

1. Vanhoozer has a most compelling and comprehensive coverage of Speech Act Theory in his book, *Is there a Meaning in this Text?* Vanhoozer operates under the assumption that the Bible is a "communicative act of a communicative agent fixed by writing" (225).
2. Keller, *Prayer: Experiencing Awe and Intimacy with God*, 52.
3. Keller, *Prayer: Experiencing Awe and Intimacy with God*, 52-4.
4. Ward, *Words of Life*, 92-3, 110-11.

> God's ongoing dynamic action through the Spirit is supremely related to the language and meanings of Scripture. In other words, as we unfold the meaning of the language of Scripture, God becomes powerfully active in our lives. The Bible is not merely information, not even just completely true information. It is "alive and active" (Heb 4:12)—God's power in verbal form. It is only as we understand the meaning of the words that God names us and shapes us and recreates us.[5]

The Bible is no ordinary book. It releases the personal active presence of God into human lives, relationships, and the world. "Revelation is not simply about grace but is itself an act of grace."[6] In other words, Scripture does not simply convey information, it gets things done. God's Word does what it says.

Therefore, understanding how God gets things done with his Word is crucial. The preacher of Scripture should prepare and proclaim sermons that cut with the grain of what God is *doing* with his Word. This kind of preaching will result in reaching and renewing lives, the home, relationships, the church, neighborhoods, communities, workplaces, all kinds of places, and the surrounding culture.

The Gospel Arc preaching model seeks to participate in what God is primarily doing in all of Scripture: revealing and releasing Jesus Christ and his comprehensive salvation into the world. In other words, Jesus Christ and his salvation comprise the ultimate subject (speech) and intent (act) in all of Scripture to be personally and corporately experienced in a living encounter by faith.

Richard Bauckham notes that a Christocentric hermeneutic and homiletic of the Bible is not new: "The church's reading of Scripture has usually presupposed its narrative unity, that is, that the whole of the Bible—or the Bible read as a whole—tells a coherent story. Any part of Scripture contributes to or illuminates in some way this one story, which is the story of God's purpose for the whole world,"[7] which is revealed from front to back (reading forward) and back to front (reading backward) in Jesus Christ.

Jesus shows up in the Bible. Jesus is experienced with the Bible by faith. Therefore, when handling the scriptures, the preacher needs to become an "intelligent mystic"[8] who listens to the text (Round 1) and then becomes an explorer of the text on a quest for its meaning (Round 2).

---

5. Keller, *Preaching: Communicating Faith in an Age of Skepticism*, 34.
6. Craddock, *Preaching*, 55.
7. Bauckham, "Reading Scripture as a Coherent Story," 38.
8. Murray, *Redemption: Accomplished and Applied*, 169.

Chapter 12

The Power of Discovering the Text's Message

EVANGELIZE YOUR BIBLE READING

Everyone's Bible reading needs to be saved. If you are still in need of being sanctified, then your Bible reading is in need of life change, too. Graeme Goldsworthy connects reading the Bible accurately (or hermeneutics) to gospel renewal: "Our ability to interpret Scripture must be saved, justified and sanctified through the gospel."[1]

Goldsworthy means not only that Jesus and his salvation comprise the Bible's own hermeneutic or interpretive lens, but also that growing in the ability to read the Bible accurately is a powerful aspect of gospel renewal. In other words, growing in the ability to both read Jesus and his salvation in all of Scripture and to experience Jesus and his salvation by faith in all of life are interrelated aspects of one's sanctification, life change, or gospel renewal.

Therefore, sanctification means not only conformity to Christ in one's character but also in one's ability to read the Bible Christocentrically. One's character, which includes the mind and hermeneutic, must undergo continual gospel renewal. Our Bible reading needs to be saved.

---

1. Goldsworthy, *Gospel-Centered Hermeneutics*, 16.

Where, however, does the freedom, motivation, and effort to pursue hermeneutical sanctification come from for the pastor, parishioner, or the church? The answer is from the gospel itself, as Goldsworthy describes,

> Any aspect of sanctification, or growth in holiness, is clouded by our ongoing sinfulness and ignorance of the truth, yet we remain secure in the knowledge of our free justification on the grounds of Christ's righteousness for us. This justification does not, as it is sometimes represented, relieve us of the motive or responsibility to strive for holiness. Indeed, our free justification provides the only legitimate grounds and the most powerful motive for such striving. Likewise, the gospel presents us with the righteousness of Jesus Christ, who, in his earthly life, perfectly interpreted the word of his Father. In so doing he justified the fallible attempts of his people to interpret the word. The justification of our hermeneutics by the perfect hermeneutics of Christ is the motivation for us to strive for hermeneutical sanctification.[2]

Believers strive to read their Bibles in a more Christ-centered or sanctified way because Jesus read, applied, theologized, communicated, and overall handled the Scriptures perfectly for them. For example, unlike the first Adam in the garden, the better Adam in the wilderness relied upon or lived by every word that came from the mouth of the Lord (Luke 4:1–13).

Therefore, Jesus' righteousness—hermeneutical, noetic, or epistemological—becomes the basis for our freedom, motivation, and effort to pursue a renewed mind not only in life but also in handling the Bible.[3] The power of the gospel for salvation (Rom 1:16) includes the renewing of the mind (Rom 12:1–2). Believers have the mind of Christ (justification) and therefore strive for the mind of Christ experientially or functionally in life and ministry (sanctification), which includes how to read and communicate the Bible (Phil 2:5).

Peter Leithart gives an example of how the ability to interpret the Scriptures must be saved. He highlights the bad habit of peeling the medium of the Bible away from the message of the Bible. In other words, separating the "husk" of the Bible's verbal expressions from the "kernel" of the Bible's meaning in an effort to make the Bible practical, which "often means

---

2. Goldsworthy, *Gospel-Centered Hermeneutics*, 18.
3. Goldsworthy, *Gospel-Centered Hermeneutics*, 60–1.

drawing moralistic conclusions from the text."[4] Leithart says conservative evangelicals routinely do this.[5]

Therefore, the verbal expressions of the Bible are discarded for what really matters—the truth or meaning. If the "husk" is separated from the "kernel," however, how does one determine the meaning of the "kernel"? Ever since the battle for the Bible in the Enlightenment, reason has assumed the authority to determine the meaning of the "kernel."[6] A key player in the battle for the Bible was a Dutch Lutheran humanist, physician, and amateur theologian named Lodewijk Meyer, who wrote about "Philosophy as the Interpreter of Holy Scripture." Leithart adds,

> Meyer's book is important because in it, he initiates a hermeneutical method that detaches the truth and meaning of Scripture from its verbal expression. For Meyer, the evident claims of the text are to be taken as true only if they are judged reasonable. Subjecting the Bible to a rational test, Meyer treats the surface of the Bible—its ordinary language, poetry, metaphor, and narrative—as dispensable. The Bible's truth is found in the rationally justifiable message and not in the rustic letter; it is the rational core that remains after the husk is removed.[7]

Our effort to interpret the greater authority of Scripture must be saved from an over dependence upon the lesser authority of reason. If this were to happen, then the sanctifying change would be immediate—namely, the end of over-trusting a wooden literalistic and rationalistic hermeneutic that pumps out moralistic messages.

The medium and the message of the Bible are married. Both, together, deliver the good news of Jesus Christ and his salvation for personal and corporate gospel renewal: "We get to the richly varied *senus plenior* of the sacramental word not by moving past the letter to a spiritual sense, not by treating the letter as a husk for removal. We get at the riches of Scripture precisely by luxuriating in the letter, by squeezing everything we can from the text as written."[8]

---

4. Leithart, *Deep Exegesis*, 30.

5. Leithart defines the "husk" of the Bible as, "the authors' word choices, structural organization, tropes and allusions, and intertextual quotations" (*Deep Exegesis*, vii). Therefore, the "husk" of the Bible is its verbal expressions or the medium by which its meaning, truth, or message is inscripturated and communicated.

6. Leithart, *Deep Exegesis*, 7.

7. Leithart, *Deep Exegesis*, 10.

8. Leithart, *Deep Exegesis*, vii.

LEARN LAW AND GOSPEL

God ultimately has two words running through his inscripturated-Word, from Genesis to Revelation: *law and gospel*.[9] These two words *do* what they *say* through the Bible's rich theological history and its vast matrix of interpenetrating ideas and images embedded in its historical, literary, and theological soil.

The Bible is a highly selective history of divine events (redemptive history) *and* a thick interpretation of those events (divine messages) that ultimately communicate law and gospel. Therefore, the Bible's narrative, poetic, apocalyptic, wisdom, and propositional literary forms ultimately communicate law and gospel. A growing fluency in law and gospel opens the Bible to us. Ignorance, confusion, and conflation of law and gospel shut the Bible to us, thereby, turning the Bible into a closed book that confines readers to their self-inflicted interpretive prisons of moralism and relativism.

What is the law? The quick answer is that which *demands*. And the demand is perfection—not trying harder, self-improvement, doing your best, or better luck next time. "Be perfect, as your heavenly Father is perfect" (Matt 5:48), period. We must be a perfect, flourishing human being to justify our existence before God, others, ourselves, the big law (God's ten moral laws) as well as the endless little laws of life.[10] We must be perfect to avoid being nothing, that is, condemned to death.

Because all of life is watched and measured by the law,[11] all of life is a trial. "Are you enough? Are you doing enough?" demands the law. Every aspect of being, doing, and relating becomes a desperate moment in the struggle for righteousness. Love and acceptance hang in the balance. Being a cosmic somebody or nobody is at stake. The age of anxiety is real. It is no accident that many myths, legends, and epic stories throughout human history involve heroic trials needing to be overcome to prove one's worth and attain glory.

Despite all effort, it is gore not glory that awaits us. Like the typical horror flick, the law leads us into the basement where accusation and condemnation lurk: "You *are* not enough. You don't *do* enough. You are *nothing*.

---

9. "Similarly, elaborating the law-gospel distinction, the Reformed tradition developed a covenant theology that distinguished between the conditional covenants sworn by the people (Adam and Israel) and the unconditional oath sworn by God (the *protoeuangelion* of Genesis 3:15 and the Abrahamic, Davidic, and new covenant)." Horton, *Justification*, 57.

10. Think of the law of productivity, a size two dress, the food you ate for lunch, your work-out routine, or the lack of work-out routine!

11. No wonder the French philosopher, Jean-Paul Sarte, likened hell to being looked at.

You *cease* to exist." And the accusations are not fictitious. Everyone asks from cradle to grave, sun up to sun down, consciously and subconsciously, "Who am I? What is my worth and value? Am I loved and accepted? What is my righteousness, my save-ability?" We desperately need answers, but the law rightly responds, "Who are you? You are condemned, down to the roots of your being. You are nothing. You are rejected. You have no righteousness. You are a corpse sealed in its tomb." Condemnation and shame are not imaginary; they are demons that haunt us all.

Adding to the exhaustion of demand, the anxiety of accusation, and the depression of condemnation is the law's inability to do anything about it. The law cannot make us heroes in our own story. It cannot activate righteousness and life in us; it cannot deliver us from condemnation and death. It cannot save us because it is unable, impotent. It is impossible; it can only perpetuate death or nothingness.

Why is the law so powerless to save? There are two reasons. First, the human condition from Genesis 3 onward is not simply *doing* sins, but is *in* sin. We *do* sins because we are *in* sin, that is, we are sinful or of the "flesh."[12] We come into this world *in* sin or of the flesh—no exceptions. Therefore, employing the law in an attempt to activate righteous and to deliver from sin's guilt and power, is like bringing a squirt gun to a gunfight in Fallujah. The law cannot save a sinner. Ironically, if the law is employed in an attempt to activate righteousness and to deliver from sin's guilt and power, then it simply becomes another addictive substance in the obsession to be one's own savior (Rom 7).

Second, the law does not possess one drop of divine life and redemptive power in it—not a drop. It expertly explains human flourishing but cannot make it happen. The law is powerless to justify, sanctify, glorify, or otherwise heal a life. Only Jesus (the gospel) is able to do the impossible. Therefore, if you read law in the Bible, you are reading, "It is never finished! Be this! Do this! I only demand." In this way, the corpse is sealed in its tomb, and the law's ministry of death is complete (2 Cor 3:7).

Even so, the law does possess one spectacular function largely ignored in our excitement to live the victorious Christian life today. When the law seals the Adamic corpse in its tomb of sin, nakedness, accusation,

12. The Apostle Paul signifies the "flesh" as the universal human condition under the reign of sin and death that entered the world as a consequence of the guilt of the original sin (Romans 5). Furthermore, Paul contrasts "flesh" and "Spirit" not only as two different human conditions or natures inherited by the work of two different Adams (Romans 5), but also as two different eschatological ages ushered in by the work of those two different Adams. The first Adam's work of disobedience produced the old age of sin and death. The better Adam's work of obedience produced the new age of righteousness and life.

condemnation, shame, death, nothingness, fear, and self-salvation, it limits comfort in life and death to one singular person—Jesus Christ.[13] Finally, we have nowhere else to go (John 6:68). Finally, we become what we have always been—nothing. It is here, in our nothingness, that we experience something truly remarkable—ourselves. Therefore, in this way we are driven out of ourselves and toward Jesus and his salvation (Gal 3). This is a spectacular work!

What is the gospel? The quick answer is that which *freely gives*. The gospel *freely gives* Jesus and his comprehensive salvation to the corpse sealed in its tomb. Therefore, the gospel gives a resurrection from the dead. It does not bark out self-improvement instructions to a corpse (Gal 3:3), but instead offers life from death and freedom from the tomb.

The gospel freely gives because Jesus satisfied both the penal demands of the law (condemnation and death) and the positive demands of the law (perfect righteousness), thereby, securing justification and life or a comprehensive salvation by grace alone. Salvation is by works—just not ours! Jesus accomplished, achieved, won, secured, earned, merited, performed, purchased, or otherwise worked salvation *for us*. No other work is needed. Salvation is finished because Jesus finished it, and the gospel freely gives Jesus and his salvation.

Therefore, the heart of the gospel is *substitution*. It is either the sinner or Jesus who is condemned (legal power) and consequently suffers comprehensive death (dynamic power). The gospel says, "It was always Jesus." It is either the sinner's filthy rags or Jesus' royal robe of righteousness that secures justification and life. The gospel says, "It was always Jesus."

Justification, sanctification, and glorification (the whole package of a comprehensive salvation) has been achieved by Jesus *for us* (substitution). Thereby, salvation is *freely given* (i.e., by grace) to the corpse sealed in its tomb. The gospel says to us, "Salvation is received not achieved, well, just not achieved by you."

Therefore, all of life is freedom for the Christian (Gal 5:1). Freedom from condemnation and the consequential enslavement to the dark powers of sin, death, and the evil one in all their multi-form prisons of misery (Rom 8:1–2). Freedom from the enslaving fear of punishment (1 John 4:18), that is, from a spirit of psychological imprisonment to fear (Rom 8:15–17). Freedom from living in the realm of the dead where the dark lords of sin, death, and personal evil tyrannically reign (Col 1:13; Rom 6:1–11). Christians are free from the age of sin and death, both legally and dynamically (Rom 8:1–2).

---

13. Heidelberg Catechism, question one.

Furthermore, all of life is freedom for the Christian (Gal 5:1) because when Jesus exited the tomb, he took us with him legally and dynamically (Rom 4:25). Legally, we are finally enough—we have finally done enough; we are perfect. We possess what every human being from Adam onward has desperately longed and strived for their whole life—justification, peace with God (Rom 5:1). Therefore, dynamically the age of the Spirit of life is ours, that is, sanctification and eventually glorification (Rom 8:1–2).

Practically speaking, peace with God means peace with ourselves, others, the law, the little laws of life, and any other demanding, accusing, and condemning power against us. Ending the struggle for righteousness truly changes a life. It sanctifies. Therefore, justification is a big deal for the *Christian*. It empowers an outward life of love and good works toward others. The resurrection of Jesus ushers in the age of the Spirit—legally and dynamically, personally and eschatologically, individually and corporately, and any other way we seem to stumble over the distinct and yet inseparable truths of the gospel.

Therefore, if you read gospel in the Bible, you are reading, "It is finished! Believe this! I freely give!" The corpse sealed in its tomb exited the tomb with Jesus into a whole new creation of righteousness and life. The gospel unleashes heaven in hell, setting the captives free. The gospel gives and gives and keeps on giving above and beyond (infinitely so) anything we could even ask for or possibly imagine (Eph 3:20–21).

Isn't There More Though?

Isn't there a "Third Word" from God beyond Law and Gospel for the Christian? Is there some kind of hybrid law-gospel cocktail in the Bible for the Christian? In other words, does the law play some kind of activating role in the Christian's sanctification, renewal, or life change? Or is the law necessarily added to the gospel (or faith) in order to sanctify a life? The answer from the Bible is, "No, hell no!"[14]

The law does not possess one drop of divine life or redemptive power in it to activate a life (Rom 8:3). If it did, then Christ died for nothing (Gal 2:21). "For what need of Christ to give Himself for him, if he without the Christ was able to be justified by his keeping of the law? Then let Christ be

---

14. See Horton, *Justification*, 57–95 for the Biblical-theological support to avoid monocovenantalism, that is, the widespread tendency to reduce (conflate) the distinct law and gospel covenants into a single type. Thereby, not only losing the divine speech acts of law and gospel in the Bible, but also unleashing chaos into one's hermeneutic, pursuit of biblical meaning, and "systematic reflection on the meaning of salvation . . . piety, mission, and life together." Horton, *Justification*, 53.

taken away with all his benefits, for He is utterly unprofitable."[15] The law has no life in it and can neither justify nor sanctify a life. It is impossible for the law to activate justification or sanctification. Therefore, the law is not the power of God for salvation, but that place is reserved only for the gospel of Jesus Christ and his salvation (Rom 1:16).

What Is the Law's Role?

If there is no life in the law, what is its role in the Christian's sanctification? The quick answer is that it describes what sanctification or believing the gospel looks like in our lives and relationships. In other words, learning to build your messy life and relationships around Jesus and his salvation or learning to walk in the Spirit (same thing) looks like loving God and loving others. The law points to what sanctification looks like, but possesses none of the power to actually make it happen. That power is reserved for the gospel alone—sanctification is by faith alone or the gospel alone.

The longer answer is that the law possesses the significant role of addressing the Adamic-self that exists in both the unbeliever (as a collapsed-self) and the believer (as a conflicted-self) in order to drive both out of themselves and toward Jesus and his salvation alone for justification and sanctification respectively (Gal 3:19–26). In other words, the law has the spectacular role of revealing our sin to us, or us to ourselves (Rom 7:7–13).

There is no life change, renewal, or sanctification for the Christian apart from any meaningful self-understanding (humility, need, repentance, pick your word). Self-understanding informs an intelligent repentance, or the honest identification of specific strategies of self-salvation still actively present in the life of the Christian. Self-understanding alone, however, does not change a life. What is needed to change a life is a living, continuous connection with Jesus and his salvation by faith. In other words, what is needed is for Jesus and his salvation to functionally address the specific forms of self-salvation that still wreck us. This is applying the gospel to our lives and relationships, and it is in this way that we change.

Therefore, the gospel is the power of God to renew the "new self . . . in knowledge after the image of its creator" (Col 3:10). The gospel produces faith in Jesus and his salvation that not only justifies but also sanctifies, that is, functionally "puts off" the old self and "puts on" the new self (Col 3:9–10).

Any strategy to activate sanctification by adding something to the gospel (like the law) is a form of self-sanctification. In other words, trying to activate God or the Holy Spirit in the Christian life beyond faith alone is

15. Luther, *Commentary on Galatians*, 119.

simply "putting on" the old self or walking around in the flesh. It is putting lipstick on a pig, or as Jesus says, a coat of paint on a tomb (Matt 23:27).

What about the Law in Sanctification?

What about it beyond its obvious role? "You shall not murder" does not cease to command a Christian. Avoiding murder does not cease to be a good thing when you become a Christian. The law does not stop pointing the way to human flourishing in God's world after you become a Christian. It is always a good thing for a human being not to murder another human being, Christian or not. Therefore, "You shall not murder" still applies to the Christian.

This is not the real issue though, is it? There seems to be an odd over-concern for the law in the Christian life today in some circles. It is this over-concern for the law in sanctification that is much more complicated.

What about the Odd Over-Concern for the Law Today?

The odd over-concern for the law in sanctification today arises from believing the law has some kind of activating power in the Christian life, that it somehow activates the Holy Spirit in the Christian for sanctification. In other words, the law activates the Holy Spirit in the Christian who *now* knows what to do and is empowered to do so.

Therefore, according to this activating view of the law, any lack of law instruction in sanctification is tantamount to licentiousness or antinomianism. The law, however, does not activate the Christian life nor the Holy Spirit in the Christian's life—only the gospel does. Why then this over-concern for the law in sanctification?

Ironically, the view that the law is an activating power in the Christian life for sanctification is exactly what Paul says is impossible in Galatians 3:1–6. Trying to "perfect yourself in the flesh" (v. 3) by the law or any form of self-activation (even with the Holy Spirit's help) is just plain "stupid" according to Paul (v. 1). Neither the law, human effort, nor any form of human-Holy Spirit cooperation is able to control, manage, kill, cure, heal, fix, rehabilitate, deliver, rescue, save, change, renew, make alive, counsel, or otherwise sanctify the "old self," sinful nature, or flesh.

First, the "old self" had to be killed, not cured. Second, it took God himself to do the killing. Third, it still does. Trying to fix yourself is an exercise in futility, anxiety, exhaustion, and depression. Trying to fix (kill and make alive) your zombie-self (the "old self," flesh, sinful nature, or indwelling sin) is impossible. It is beyond our powers. Furthermore, the "old self" will never enter the kingdom of God (Eph 5:5) because it has no place among the living. It is only ever condemned to death, either at the cross or at final judgment.

Therefore, biblical life change, renewal, or sanctification not only involves the killing of the "old self" by the death of Jesus, but also the gracious addition or gift of a "new self" by the resurrection of Jesus. This is why Jesus told Nicodemus, "Truly, truly, I say to you, unless one is born of water and the Spirit, he cannot enter the kingdom of God. That which is born of flesh is flesh, and that which is born of Spirit is spirit. Do not marvel that I say to you, 'You must be born again'" (John 3:5–7).

This is why the Apostle Paul informs the Christian of their sanctification by saying, "But now we are released from the law, having died to that which held us captive, so that we serve in the new way of the Spirit and not in the old way of the written code" (Rom 7:6). Stunningly, Paul implies that serving in the old way of the written code (or law) is the way of the flesh, that is, of the sinful nature or "old self." Is the over-concern for the law in sanctification trying to promote this?

The legal source and dynamic power of life change, renewal, or sanctification is only and always the life, death, and resurrection of Jesus. Living by faith in the present power of the life, death, and resurrection of Jesus is sanctifying—it is living by the Spirit; it is the gospel's way of life. "I am the way, the truth, and the life" (John 14:6).

In contrast, living by faith in the law and/or other forms of self-activation is the law's way of death; it is living by the flesh. "For those who live according to the flesh set their minds on the things of the flesh, but those who live according to the Spirit set their minds on the things of the Spirit" (Rom 8:5). Therefore, set your mind on the things of the Spirit, that is, the present power of the life, death, and resurrection of Jesus Christ for your sanctification, renewal, or life change.

It is important to note that the over-concern for the law in sanctification does not originate in a concern for the so called "third use" of the law, but rather in something else entirely. It originates from a whole new classification for the law: a "third word" from God for the Christian. In other words, when the law is believed to activate a Christian's sanctification or to activate the Holy Spirit in the Christian for sanctification, then we are no longer talking about a "third *use*" of the law but rather a "third *word*" from God beyond law and gospel.

Therefore, the odd overconcern for the law in sanctification today is based upon a faulty activating view of the law in the Christian life. Yet the law has no life in it. It does not possess any activating power to sanctify or to activate the Holy Spirit in the Christian for sanctification.

Practically speaking, whenever the law, biblical principles, exhortations, commands, invitations, warnings, rebukes, or calls to obedience are employed in biblical communication and ministry without any *meaningful connection* to the gospel as the only power of God for sanctification (i.e., the only activating power or source in the Christian life), then a "third word" from God is functionally experienced by those who hear it. In other words, some form of: "I can activate my sanctification by the law and so can you"; or "The law activates the Holy Spirit within me—who now knows what to do and empowers me to do it." Activating sanctification by the law (with or without the Holy Spirit's help) is a functional "third word" from God for the Christian. Since there is no such thing, however, the result is simply another form of self-sanctification run amok.

A quick response to the over-concern for the law in sanctification today is the following. First, the law does not carry one drop of divine life or sanctifying power in it. It does not activate sanctification nor the Holy Spirit living in the Christian for sanctification. In other words, there is no "third word" from God for the Christian. Second, "You shall not murder" works pretty well for the Christian, too. Third, God's two words of law and gospel do not need any extra help in the Christian's life. They are divinely sufficient for the Holy Spirit's work in the life of the Christian. They are immediately relevant for any and all human conditions found not only in the world but also in the church.

Perhaps ultimately, the issue can be resolved by answering the simple question: does the law carry one drop of divine life and sanctifying power in it? Your answer determines how you handle the law in sanctification, renewal, or life change. If yes, then the law is handled "unlawfully" (1 Tim 1:8–9). It is handled in a moralistic or self-activating way. If no, then the law is handled "lawfully" (1 Tim 1:8–9). It is handled in a way that serves the gospel.

How does the law serve the gospel? The answer is by driving the Christian experientially out of themselves (i.e., out of all the functional strategies of human effort still within) and toward Jesus and his salvation ever anew and afresh.

The gospel alone sanctifies or activates the Holy Spirit in the Christian for sanctification, while the law plays the servant who leads us out of ourselves and toward Jesus and his salvation. The over-concern for the law in sanctification is a misplaced concern.

What about the So-Called "Third Use of the law"?

First, the traditional language is unfortunate since it can be easily manipulated into a "third word" from God for the Christian, which does not exist. Notice, however, it is a third *use* of the law not a third *word* from God.

Second, the language communicates that the law has a much more positive contribution to make to sanctification than actually corresponds to reality. The "third use of the law," properly understood, simply and only possesses descriptive power in sanctification. In other words, it describes or instructs what life change or a flourishing life looks like while possessing none of the power to make it happen.

Therefore, the "third use of the law" instructs that sanctification looks like love. It looks like loving God and loving others. Still, ironically, it is the gospel, not the "third use of law," that *fully* interprets and instructs what loving God and loving others looks like. For example, it is Jesus (the gospel himself) in Matthew 5 who plunges to the bottom of the human heart to fully and finally interpret the law or love for us. Furthermore, it is the Apostle Paul at the end of his letters who fully and finally *patterns* the relational dynamics of love upon Jesus' self-giving life, death, and resurrection. In this way, the gospel fully develops what love looks like or gives love its final and full interpretation or description.

Third, the descriptive function of the "third use of the law" is well, underwhelming; it is redundant. The law is already written on the human heart and life (Rom 1–2). It is inherent to being a human being or image-bearer; it is embedded in every person. In other words, the law is part of the DNA of being human and therefore for human flourishing. This means human beings already know the law on the *inside*—even as it is being suppressed (Rom 1). Therefore, the "third use of the law" provides the unspectacular function of reminding us of what we already know.

Fourth, once the "third use of the law" reminds us to love God and love others, it must then defer to the only power that can actually do something about it—the gospel. If the "third use of the law" does not defer to the gospel to sanctify, renew, or change a life, then it sinks in the swamp of self-sanctification (moralistic life change). Therefore, for these four reasons, caution should be exercised against any over-enthusiastic approaches of the "third use of the law" in sanctification.

What Is the More Spectacular Function of the Law?

What is the more spectacular function of the law in Sanctification? The answer is the law's ability to reveal the hiddenness and hideousness of sin in our lives and relationships (Rom 7).[16] Why is this work of sealing the corpse of the old-self in its tomb so crucial? The answer is once sealed in the tomb, Jesus' life, death, and resurrection becomes absolutely spectacular! The law serves the sin-killing and life-giving power of the gospel in the Christian's life by convincing us of the utter impossibility of perfecting ourselves in the flesh, that is, of being our own savior (Gal 3).

Therefore, the law's primary power and function is to kill, accuse, curse, demand, imprison, reveal, crush, judge, measure, evaluate, watch, condemn, lead to despair, and to otherwise show the utter impossibility of the Adamic-self (old self) to justify and sanctify itself. The law has the ability to convince us of our complete inability to be our own lord and savior. In this primary and powerful way, the law drives us out of ourselves and toward Jesus and his salvation alone. This is what Jesus means by self-denial and picking up your cross. "Self-denial is not negative: it is positive re-direction of the total being."[17]

This is a spectacular work! And it is this incredible work of the law that is desperately needed in sanctification. We need a true understanding of ourselves to be sanctified. We need the law to reveal us to us. We need the smelling-salt of the law to clear our head about ourselves, namely, our delusions of self-salvation.

What about Imperatives and Exhortations in Sanctification?

Of course, gospel life change involves teaching, persuading, inviting, warning, correcting, rebuking, training, coaching, or otherwise applying God's two words of law and gospel to messy lives and real relationships. Applying the law and gospel to the human condition certainly involves a full spectrum of interpersonal communication.

At the same time, it is crucial to recognize that the full spectrum of interpersonal communication functions properly within the context of rightly applying the law (imperative) and the gospel (indicative). Teaching, persuading, inviting, warning, correcting, rebuking, training, and coaching, and so on form their communicative intent (human speech act) within the meta-intent of law and gospel (divine speech act).

---

16. Keller, *War Between Your Selves*.
17. Berkouwer, *Studies In Dogmatics*, 139.

Therefore, if various modes of interpersonal communication are disconnected from the meta-intent of law and gospel, they become confusing at best and moralistic at worst. It seems that a full spectrum of interpersonal communication built around the meta-intent of law and gospel ultimately will be informed and shaped by: 1) the presenting human condition, 2) applying the law to the presenting human condition, 3) applying the gospel to the presenting human condition, and 4) unpacking the implications of believing the gospel in life and relationships in light of the presenting human condition. In other words, unpacking the implications for how the gospel re-enchants life.

Chapter 13

The Power of Discovering the Textual Jesus

MAKE GOD A MEANINGFUL AUTHOR OF THE BIBLE

How many authors of the Bible are there? Who is the real author of the Bible? Keller notes four competing views of biblical authorship that wrestle with the tension of authorial intent in the Bible: 1) the human author only view (liberal view), 2) the divine author only view (allegorical view), 3) the divinely inspired human author only view (conservative evangelical view), and 4) the double authorship view (Christocentric evangelical view).[1]

The Absent Author

In this view, God is not an author of the Bible. The human author only view (liberal view) either rejects divine authorship formally or functionally. In other words, God is the "Absent Author" of the Bible.

When human authorship jettisons any meaningful divine authorship, then the canonical context or unified message of the Bible is lost. When Moses says one thing, David another, and then Luke and Paul still something

---

1. Keller and Clowney, "Preaching Christ in a Postmodern World."

else, the unity of the Bible is lost. Without a divine author, there is no ultimate metanarrative of the Bible to integrate the messages from each of the human authors.

Furthermore, any effort to systematize significant biblical ideas are impossible before the impenetrable theological silos of Moses, David, Luke, Paul, et al. Therefore, the aim of the human author only view of the Bible is to discover each human author's single autonomous intent.[2]

The Lonely Author

In this view, God is the only author of the Bible. The divine author only view (allegorical view) either rejects human authorship formally or functionally. In other words, God is the "Lonely Author" of the Bible.

When divine authorship jettisons any meaningful human authorship, then the human and the historical become irrelevant. Therefore, an allegorical or woodenly literal approach to the Bible prevails, rending revelation from its historical embodiment[3] and producing "no real historical or theological connection between the text and its spiritual meaning."[4]

In the divine author only view, the human author's intent, or the original historical meaning, is non-existent or avoided for a "deeper spiritual meaning"[5] hidden in the text. Therefore, the aim of the divine author only view is to discover the deeper spiritual meaning in the text. This is done not only without the aid of the human author, but also only with the aid of the human reader, in the form of their imagination and/or special revelatory anointing of the Holy Spirit. In this way, the interpretation of the text is as open as the reader's imagination.

The "Ghost Writer"

In this view, God only inspired the human authors. He is not an author himself in any meaningful way. In other words, God is a "Ghost Writer" of the Bible.

The human author's single conscious intent is all that matters.[6] The divinely inspired human author only view (conservative evangelical view)

---

2. Keller and Clowney, "Preaching Christ in a Postmodern World."
3. Keller and Clowney, "Preaching Christ in a Postmodern World."
4. Goldsworthy, *Preaching the Whole Bible as Christian Scripture*, 77.
5. Goldsworthy, *Preaching the Whole Bible as Christian Scripture*, 77.
6. Goldsworthy, *Preaching the Whole Bible as Christian Scripture*, 77.

is most commonly associated with a "non-Christocentric evangelical approach."[7] Therefore, the human author's single conscious intent is not only God's intent but also only God's intent, as Walter Kaiser observes,

> Only one verbal meaning is to be connected with any passage of Scripture. . . . The Spirit takes the single truth-intention of the author . . . Nowhere, then, does Scripture support the view that the Bible has a multi-track concept of meanings. If the human author did not receive by revelation the meaning in question, then exegetes and readers have no right to identify their meanings with God.[8]

The divinely inspired human author only view claims pure objective exegetical support in its pursuit of textual meaning, whereas the double authorship view, it claims, is too subjective or speculative. For Keller, the divinely inspired human author only view suffers from being "just as speculative" as the double author view.[9]

For example, in seeking to discover the original historical meaning of a passage, some interpreters see the human author knowing more than others, while other interpreters see the human author knowing less.[10] Philip Payne notes the inevitability of context and the challenge it provides: "The exegete who limits his discussion of the meaning of a passage to what he is convinced was the intention of the author will produce a different kind of exegesis than the exegete who lets the text within its total context determine the meaning."[11] Therefore, when working with a text, both the textual intent and the inevitable contextual intent wrestle with objective and subjective elements of interpretation.

Poythress presses further by noting that even if readers "confine [themselves] to people who hold to the classic doctrine of inspiration . . . [as] both God's word and the word of the human authors . . . we still do not have agreement about the relation of God's meaning to the meaning of the human author."[12] Citing Darrell Bock's research, Vern Poythress counts "no less than four distinct approaches among evangelicals" attempting to work out the relation of meaning between God's meaning and the human author's meaning.[13]

7. Keller and Clowney, "Preaching Christ in a Postmodern World."
8. Kaiser, "Single Intent of Scripture," 66–7, 69.
9. Keller and Clowney, "Preaching Christ in a Postmodern World."
10. Keller and Clowney, "Preaching Christ in a Postmodern World."
11. Payne, "Fallacy of Equating Meaning with the Human Author's Intention," 80, footnote 19.
12. Poythress, "Divine Meaning of Scripture," 83.
13. Poythress, "Divine Meaning of Scripture," 83.

There will always be both objective and subjective elements involved in interpreting the human and the divine intent of any given passage of the Bible. Therefore, to reject the double authorship view based on the presupposition that the human intention inherently possesses superior properties of objectivity over the divine intention is unfounded.

The Meaningful Author

In this view, God is a meaningful author of the Bible in his own right. The double author view of the Bible is closely connected to a "Christocentric approach to the Bible."[14] The double author view understands the Bible to have two authors, the human and the divine, both of whom authored the Bible in a dynamic process of inspiration.[15]

The dynamic of the double authoring process preserves the concept of divine intention through human intention as well as divine intention beyond human intention in terms of correspondence, escalation, and overall unity. The ultimate divine intention completes the original human intention yet does not contradict it. The reason, Greidanus asserts, is that God not only worked sovereignly in human history and salvation history, but also in the historical inscripturation process of the Scriptures.[16] In other words, God is a meaningful author in his own right.

A TRUE UNDERSTANDING, NOT AN EXHAUSTIVE UNDERSTANDING

Did the human authors fully grasp the divine intention in their historical writings at every turn? The answer is they had a true understanding of what they wrote but not an exhaustive one. The incomplete or partial

---

14. Keller and Clowney, "Preaching Christ in a Postmodern World."

15. The importance of biblical inspiration (2 Timothy 3:16; 2 Peter 1:20–21; John 16:12–15) lies in the divine origin of the words or speech acts rather than in the precise manner of its authoring. Ward writes, "All major Reformed writers on the topic, from Calvin through to Warfield, are agreed that the main thrust of the doctrine of inspiration is that the words of Scripture have their origin in God. Whether the focus of interest is the means by which God acted in the production of Scripture should be on prior events in the writer's life, where God through the Spirit spoke to him words he later wrote, or on the actual moment of composition, is a secondary matter, over which differences of emphasis do not count for a great deal . . . in the seventeenth and eighteenth centuries too much speculation arose in some quarters over the mechanics of divine authorship through human authors" (Ward, *Words of Life*, 82).

16. Greidanus, *Preaching Christ from the Old Testament*, 249.

understanding of the human author means God had an authorial intent that must be considered, whether the human author was conscious of it or not.

Raymond Brown calls this gap in the text between the human author's conscious intention and God's intention the *sensus plenior*: "that additional, deeper meaning, intended by God but not clearly intended by the human author, which is seen to exist in the words of a biblical text (or group of texts, or even a whole book) when they are studied in the light of further revelation or development in the understanding of revelation."[17] Greidanus provides an example of *sensus plenior* in Numbers 21, noting that Moses was not likely to know that in "relating the story of the bronze serpent he was sketching a type of Christ. The type in this passage is discovered only from the New Testament perspective when Jesus makes use of this event to proclaim his own saving work."[18]

Philip Payne presses the point by noting not only the gap in the text between the human author's intention and God's intention, but also in the understanding of the human author: "the scriptural text seems to teach that at least in certain instances the biblical writer was not aware of the full import of his own words . . . there were certain things the biblical writers conveyed that they themselves did not fully understand."[19]

Scripture as the Inscripturation of Redemptive History

Does the double author view avoid allegory when it argues for a *sensus plenior*, a gap in authorial understanding and intention that can occur at times between the human author and God? In other words, does the double author view avoid the original historical meaning of the human author at times for some deeper divine meaning beyond the original text?

The answer is the double author view not only establishes the original historical meaning of the text, but also the ultimate historical meaning of the text, which is the life, death, and resurrection of Jesus Christ. The original historical meaning of the human author is integrated into the ultimate redemptive-historical meaning of the divine author. In this way, the double author view establishes God's sovereign authorship of redemptive history and its inscripturation through multiple human authors in various

17. Brown, *Sensus Plenior of Sacred Scripture*, 92.
18. Greidanus, *Preaching Christ from the Old Testament*, 233.
19. Payne, "Fallacy of Equating Meaning with the Human Author's Intention," 76–7. Payne notes Daniel 8:27 where Daniel says he was not only appalled by the vision God gave him but also "did not understand it." Payne also cites Abraham (Gen 22:8) and Caiaphas (John 11:51) of speaking better than they knew.

historical contexts. Therefore, the double author view is decidedly both historical and theological.

Furthermore, redemptive history is not static, segmented, or limited to a specific human author within a specific point in time.[20] Rather, redemptive history unfolds progressively and dynamically by means of multiple authors covering thousands of years that ultimately culminate in the person and work of Jesus Christ. Geerhardus Vos likens the progressive nature of redemptive history and its inscripturation to a seed: "The progressive process is organic: revelation may be in seed form which yields later full growth accounting for diversity but not true difference because the earlier aspects of the truth are indispensable for understanding the true meanings of the later forms and vice versa."[21]

Therefore, the double author view does not avoid the original historical meaning as in allegory, nor isolate the original historical meaning from redemptive history as in the divinely inspired human author only view. Rather, the double author view establishes the original historical meaning and then integrates it into redemptive history, thereby accounting for both human authorship and God's sovereign authorship converging in the inscripturation of redemptive history. The double author view arises out of the nature of Scripture itself as the inscripturation of redemptive history, not the avoidance of it.

The Central Figure of Redemptive History

The double author view of the Bible not only best accounts for the nature of Scripture as the inscripturation of redemptive history, but also for the inscripturation of the central figure in redemptive history, as Sidney Greidanus captures:

> The unity of redemptive history implies the Christocentric nature of every historical text. Redemptive history is the history of Christ. He stands at its center, but no less at its beginning and end . . . Scripture discloses the theme, the scope of its historiography right at the beginning. "Genesis 3.15," Veer says, "places all subsequent events in the light of the tremendous battle between Christ coming into the world and Satan the ruler of this world, and it places all events in the light of the complete victory which

---

20. Historical silos happen by default in the divinely inspired human author only view due to meaning being restricted to each human author's conscious historical field of vision.

21. Vos, *Biblical Theology*, 7.

the Seed of the woman shall attain. In view of this, it is imperative that not one single person be isolated from this history and set apart from this great battle. The place of both opponents and co-workers can only be determined Christologically. Only insofar as they received their place and task in the development of this history do they appear in the historiography of Scripture. From this point of view the facts are selected and recorded."[22]

If Jesus Christ is the central figure of redemptive history and the Bible is the inscripturation of redemptive history, then the Bible inherently must be Christocentric.

Therefore, a Christocentric reading of an Old Testament event, per Greidanus, is "simply understanding this event in its full redemptive-historical context. Moreover, even though we discover this fuller meaning only retrospectively from a later stage of redemptive history, from God's perspective it was always there in his overall design of redemptive history."[23]

Richard Hays agrees and sees a retrospective gospel lens picking up the original historical signifiers embedded in the original historical meaning by a God "who had scripted the whole biblical drama in such a way that it had multiple senses. Some of these senses are hidden, so that they come into focus only retrospectively . . . in light of Jesus' life, death, and resurrection."[24] He posits that a retrospective reading of the Bible highlights God's ultimate intention or speech act being Jesus Christ and his salvation:

> The Evangelists were convinced that the events of Jesus' life and death and resurrection were in fact revelatory: they disclosed the key to understanding all that had gone before. Of course, this involves reassessment and transformation. After the resurrection, the community of Jesus' followers returns to reread Scripture under the guidance of the Spirit and experiences, again and again, an "Aha!" reaction. Their eyes were opened anew."[25]

The double author view accounts for God sovereignly designing and imbedding in Israel's history (or Old Testament revelation) a vast matrix of meaning that signifies not only itself in its own original historical context, but also God's final and full revelation of Jesus Christ and his salvation. The human authors may or may not have possessed exhaustive understanding of what they wrote at any given time, but God always did.

---

22. Greidanus, *Sola Scriptura*, 135.
23. Greidanus, *Sola Scriptura*, 252.
24. Hays, *Reading Backwards*, 104, and Hays, *Echoes of Scripture in the Gospels*, 348.
25. Hays, *Reading Backwards*, 104–5.

Therefore, biblical hermeneutics involves pursuing an interpretive arc between the two poles of: 1) the human author's original historical meaning, and 2) the divine author's progressive revelation culminating in the final and full meaning of Jesus Christ and his salvation. Biblical accuracy means reading both forward from the text to Jesus Christ and his salvation and backwards (retrospectively) from Jesus Christ and his salvation to the text. This dual reading of the Bible recognizes that "intertextual semantic effects can flow both directions: an earlier text can illuminate a later one and vice versa."[26]

The Odd Couple

Hays points out that modern criticism and evangelical hermeneutics today are an odd couple. They both possess the same hermeneutical position that the "only legitimate interpretation of the Old Testament is strictly constrained to the original historical meaning of the Hebrew authors."[27] Therefore, they both declare "*a priori* that the Gospel writers were wrong and misguided and that their claims to revelatory retrospective reading are false."[28]

Whether it is the modern critic "debunking the Gospel's interpretations of the Old Testament," or the evangelical "contending desperately that the authors of the Old Testament's narratives and poems actually did intentionally forecast the details of Jesus' life," both work from the "rationalistic historicism of high modernity"[29] rather than from a robust double author view of the Bible. Therefore, both confine biblical meaning to the human author's conscious intent, thereby functionally avoiding any meaningful divine authorship.

Double Authorship Conclusion

The double author view best accounts for the working tension between the human author's intention and the divine author's intention, not only in any given passage, but also by accounting for the progressive unfolding of redemptive history and its inscripturation. The dynamic of the double authoring process preserves both divine intention through human intention and divine intention beyond human intention in terms of correspondence,

---

26. Hays, *Echoes of Scripture in the Gospels*, 347.
27. Hays, *Echoes of Scripture in the Gospels*, 359.
28. Hays, *Echoes of Scripture in the Gospels*, 359.
29. Hays, *Echoes of Scripture in the Gospels*, 359.

escalation, fulfillment, and overall unity. Frederick Bruner summarizes the merits of double authorship this way: "Historical-critical exegesis honors the humanity of Scripture; theological exegesis honors Scripture's divinity. Historical exegesis can keep us honest; theological exegesis can keep us relevant."[30] Taking Jesus with you to read the Bible changes everything.

READ THE BIBLE WITH JESUS AND THE NEW TESTAMENT WRITERS

How did Jesus and the New Testament writers read the Bible? They read the Scriptures retrospectively through the new or final revelatory lens of Jesus Christ's life, death, and resurrection. The revelatory act of Jesus Christ and his resurrection changed everything, including how they read their Bible.

Read Scripture with Jesus

How did Jesus read the Bible? Summarizing the textual evidence from the gospels, R. T. France answers:

> He (Jesus) uses persons in the Old Testament as types of himself (David, Solomon, Elijah, Elisha, Isaiah, Jonah) . . . he refers to Old Testament institutions as types of himself and his work (the priesthood and the covenant); he sees in the experiences of Israel foreshadowings of his own; he finds the hopes of Israel fulfilled in himself.[31]

According to France, Jesus read the Bible in light of himself. Therefore, the person and work of Jesus Christ is the optic key for understanding, applying, and communicating the Scriptures accurately. Luke 24:13–47 and John 5:39–47 are two classic passages highlighting Jesus' own exposition of the Scriptures in the light of himself.

Luke 24:13–47

Luke 24:13–47 unfolds with one unexpected event after another, climaxing with a Bible study led by the risen Redeemer. In Luke's account, the recently risen and yet unrecognized Jesus meets Cleopas and his unnamed friend on the road to Emmaus. The suspenseful twist in the story revolves around

---

30. Bruner, *Matthew Commentary*, 33.
31. France, *Jesus and the Old Testament*, 75.

how Jesus will reveal himself to these downcast and dim-sighted disciples. Will Jesus reveal himself by way of a new heavenly vision from beyond the grave?[32] "Do you see me now?!" Or will Jesus encounter them directly by insisting, "Hey fellas, it's me! Really!"

No, Jesus reaches them by having a Bible Study. Who saw that coming?! Jesus reaches them by simply sharing the Scriptures with them:

> And he said to them, "O foolish ones, and slow of heart to believe all that the prophets have spoken! Was it not necessary that the Christ should suffer these things and enter into his glory?" And beginning with Moses and all the Prophets, he interpreted to them in all the Scriptures the things concerning himself. (Luke 24:25–7)

> And their eyes were opened, and they recognized him. . . . They said to each other, "Did not our hearts burn within us while he talked to us on the road, while he opened to us the Scriptures?" (Luke 24:31–2)

Therefore, in Luke's record of the first resurrection appearance, Jesus' primary reaching and renewing pattern for the church has been established: he reveals himself and his salvation in and with the Scriptures. Experiencing Jesus with the Bible as opposed to with a direct miracle, church tradition, special anointed individual, biblical principle, or direct encounter to the heart is a big deal.

Predating the New Testament, the Scriptures with which Jesus works are the Old Testament Scriptures. Therefore, he solidifies his role as the ultimate "exegete of the biblical story" and the "definitive interpreter" of the Old Testament.[33] James Edwards summarizes Jesus' approach to reading the Bible as presenting "himself as the fulfillment of Scripture, and his life as both the interpretation and actualization of Scripture (vv. 27, 44–45)."[34]

Three interpretive dynamics are worth noting in Jesus' approach to "opening" the Scriptures to the two Emmaus disciples. First, he does not rebuke them for their failure to understand and believe his own words and predictions about his death and resurrection. Rather, he rebukes them for their failure to understand and to "believe all that the prophets have spoken" about him and his salvation.[35] The rebuke is real, not imagined, because Jesus assumes that every single prophet with whom they were familiar spoke

---

32. Hays, *Reading Backwards*, 14.
33. Hays, *Reading Backwards*, 13.
34. Edwards, *Gospel According to Luke*, 714.
35. Hays, *Reading Backwards*, 14.

of him and his salvation. Therefore, they did not understand the Bible as well as they thought. Rather, they were "foolish ones, and slow of heart to believe all that the prophets have spoken" (Luke 24:25).

Second, Jesus sees "all the Scriptures" (v. 27) bearing witness to him, not just a few carefully selected proof texts. Therefore, "the whole story of Israel builds to its narrative climax in Jesus. That is what Jesus teaches them on the road."[36] Jesus assumes an inherent hermeneutical witness to him in all the Old Testament Scriptures, both in its summary and in its parts.

Third, Jesus rereads or re-narrates the Bible for them. In other words, he "interpreted to them" the Scriptures (v. 27) or "opened" them (v. 32) from two directions: 1) he read forward from Scripture to himself, and 2) he read backwards from himself to Scripture. Jesus read forward from the Scriptures to himself because "Scripture forms the matrix within which the recent shattering events in Jerusalem become intelligible. . . . Jesus cannot be understood apart from Jewish scripture."[37] Jesus read backwards from his life, death, and resurrection to the Scriptures because "Jewish scripture cannot be understood apart from Jesus."[38]

Hays notes that reading forward from the Scriptures to Jesus Christ and his salvation and reading backwards from Jesus Christ and his salvation to the Scriptures forms an "integrative interpretation," an "intertextual interpretation," or a "figural correspondence."[39] This "intertextual interpretation" exists because the original historical meaning of the Old Testament Scriptures signifies not only itself, but also (both/and) the final and full revelation of Jesus Christ and his salvation.

How does the original historical meaning of an Old Testament passage signify not only itself but also Jesus Christ and his salvation? The answer Jesus gives from Luke 24 is Moses, all the prophets, and the Psalms carry within them a surplus of meaning divinely embedded by God. The surplus of meaning is not only capable of signifying the original historical textual meaning but also the redemptive-historical contextual meaning. The surplus of meaning is hidden, partial, or incomplete until the new revelatory light or lens of Jesus Christ and his resurrection arrives, thereby fully "opening" the Scriptures (see also Heb 1:1).

Therefore, the final and full revelation of Jesus Christ and his salvation completes a pattern of revelatory correspondence and unity that began in

36. Hays, *Reading Backwards*, 14.
37. Hays, *Reading Backwards*, 14, and Hays quoting Moberly, *Bible, Theology, and Faith*, 51.
38. Moberly, *Bible, Theology, and Faith*, 51.
39. Hays, *Reading Backwards*, 2.

the Old Testament Scriptures. The arrival of the new revelatory gospel lens now retrospectively rereads or re-narrates all previous revelation. This explains why the puzzled Emmaus disciples had all the facts of their familiarity with the Old Testament, Jesus' own teaching, their own witness of Jesus' life and works, the report of the empty tomb, and the angelic report of the resurrection, but still could not make any sense of it all. They were missing the new and final revelatory light or lens of Jesus' resurrection. They were missing the new and final revelatory pole of a figural correspondence.

Therefore, with the final revelatory lens of Jesus Christ and his salvation in place (gospel lens), Jesus retrospectively rereads the Scriptures to them. The result is their hearts burned within them "as he opened to [them] the Scriptures" (v. 32). Hays summarizes Jesus' "intertextual interpretation" of the Scriptures as providing hermeneutical unity and sanity:

> Once the pattern of correspondence has been grasped, the semantic force of the figure flows both ways, as the second event receives deeper significance from the first. For that reason, a hermeneutical strategy that relies on figural interpretation of the Bible creates deep theological coherence within the biblical narrative; it "sets forth the unity of the canon as a single cumulative and complex pattern of meaning."[40]

John 5:39–47

In this passage is found Jesus' fundamental hermeneutical claim in his own words. Furthermore, he illuminates, as Hays puts it, "John's approach to reading Israel's Scripture"[41]:

> You search the Scriptures because you think that in them you have eternal life; and it is they that bear witness about me, yet you refuse to come to me that you may have life. . . . Do not think that I will accuse you to the Father. There is one who accuses you: Moses, on whom you have set your hope. For if you believed Moses, you would believe me; for he wrote of me. But if you do not believe his writings, how will you believe my words? (John 5:39–40, 45–7).

---

40. Hays, *Echoes of Scripture in the Gospels*, 3, and quoting Frei, *Eclipse of Biblical Narrative*, 33.

41. Hays, *Echoes of Scripture in the Gospels*, 282.

Moses wrote of Jesus. Despite their rigorous study and teaching of the Scriptures, the religious leaders were exercising "interpretive failure."[42] They failed to see Jesus Christ as "the true and ultimate referent to whom Moses' words point."[43]

Once again, Jesus asserts a surplus of meaning in the Old Testament Scriptures, in this case Moses' writings. The surplus of meaning signifies not only its own original historical meaning but also Jesus Christ and his salvation. Therefore, according to Jesus, understanding the original historical meaning is not enough, and setting one's interpretive hope on Moses or David is not enough (v. 45). In other words, "Pole 1" with reference to the Gospel Arc is not enough. One must hermeneutically connect or integrate Moses' or David's original historical meaning (Pole 1) to the ultimate redemptive-historical meaning in Jesus Christ and his salvation (Pole 2). When this dual authorial intent is pursued, then the biblical text is truly understood, applied, and communicated. Otherwise, "interpretive failure" results, tending toward empty moralistic expositions.

How much did Moses know about Jesus Christ and his salvation when he wrote? The answer is enough to accuse the religious leaders of avoiding Jesus and his salvation in his writings (John 5:45). What Moses knew was true, even though it was not exhaustive.[44] Various facets of Moses's writings reveal various facets of Jesus Christ and his salvation. Each revealed facet of Jesus Christ and his salvation in Moses' writings releases the power of God for salvation upon the hearer. This helps to understand why Jesus says that Moses' writings "bear witness about me" (v. 40). Moses' writings become the occasion and the location for personally encountering Jesus Christ and his salvation. Therefore, the personal active presence of Jesus Christ and his salvation is released in Moses' writings.

In conclusion, the aim of the Old Testament Scriptures, according to Jesus in John 5:39–47, is to encounter him and his salvation or to experience him with the Bible. John 5:39–47 records Jesus inserting himself into the Bible in a corresponding, fulfilling, escalating, or completing revelatory way. Jesus Christ and his salvation retrospectively reinterprets all previous

---

42. Hays, *Echoes of Scripture in the Gospels*, 283.
43. Hays, *Echoes of Scripture in the Gospels*, 283.
44. Did Moses know exhaustively what David knew? Doubtful. Therefore, even as we move through redemptive history, there is an apparent gap in revelatory knowledge between an earlier human author and a later one. There is no gap, however, in the revelatory knowledge of the divine author who sovereignly orchestrated not only the unfolding redemptive-historical events that culminate in the event of Jesus Christ and his salvation, but also the inscripturation of those events.

revelation, so that we "come to [him] that [we] may have life" (v. 40), even in the writings of Moses.

READ SCRIPTURE WITH THE GOSPEL WRITERS

Is the Old Testament silent about Jesus Christ? The Gospel writers do not think so, since all four of them "assert that the resurrection of Jesus from the dead actually provides the hermeneutical clue that decisively integrates Israel's entire system of meaning formation."[45] The following explores how each gospel writer retrospectively reads the Old Testament Scriptures through the lens of the person and work of Jesus Christ and yet does so with his own interpretive voice.

Read a Transfigured Scripture with Matthew

Matthew's voice is prophetically explicit as he both predicts and expounds with clarity Jesus Christ and his salvation from the Old Testament Scriptures. For Matthew, Jesus is the ultimate interpreter and fulfiller of Israel's story, and thus he transfigures Israel's story: "Do not think that I have come to abolish the Law or the Prophets; I have not come to abolish them but to fulfill them" (Matt 5:17). Jesus carries Israel's story forward, thereby reconfiguring both Israel and the Torah.[46] As Richard Burridge observes, Matthew moves Jesus

> around the river Jordan, the wilderness, and the mountain—all immediately reminding us of the stories in Exodus. . . . Matthew carefully and cleverly draws his portrait of Jesus as another Moses, the new Teacher of Israel—but with one further geographical point. While Moses is shown the land of Israel from his mountain (Deut 34:1–4), Jesus sees "all the kingdoms of the world" (Matt 4:8).[47]

The early church embraced Matthew's explicit prophetic reading of Scripture by emphasizing Jesus' fulfillment not only of the direct prophecies originating in Israel, but also of Israel's own historical experiences.[48] The entire Old Testament for Matthew, both its narrative history and theological exposition, intentionally prefigures Jesus Christ and his salvation.

45. Hays, *Echoes of Scripture in the Gospels*, 3.
46. Hays, *Echoes of Scripture in the Gospels*, 351.
47. Burridge, *Four Gospels, One Jesus?*, 72–3.
48. Osbourne and Arnold, eds., *Matthew*, 184.

Furthermore, this prefiguration does not devalue Israel's story but rather front-loads it with the highest potency of value, since it is divinely and therefore inherently connected to the story of Jesus Christ and his salvation. Hays adds,

> All of Scripture is a great coherent story in which the elements of Israel's past point toward a messianic consummation.... This consummation transfigures the story that has gone before, and the hermeneutically transfigured story of Israel remains for Matthew a constitutive intertext, a *Grundgeschichte* that serves as the primary matrix for the story of Jesus.[49]

At the same time, Jesus is more than Israel 2.0, as Burridge explains, "He is all that the great heroes were—and more. He fulfills Israel's history and scriptures, law and prophets. He is the Teacher, the son of Abraham, the Davidic Messiah-King, the Lord, the Son of God himself, present with his people."[50] Jesus is the new wine bursting the old wine skins.

Read a Mysterious Scripture with Mark

Mark's voice is mysteriously veiled in his reading of the Old Testament Scriptures. He employs language "rich in symbolic vocabulary"[51] and with "cryptic scriptural pointers"[52] to unfold the "awesome mystery"[53] that is Jesus Christ. Hays expounds, "Mark's hermeneutical strategy, therefore, is to provide cryptic scriptural pointers that draw the discerning reader into the heart of the eschatological mystery."[54] Thus, whoever has ears to hear and eyes to see, per the familiar passage, will connect or integrate the original historical meaning of the Old Testament to Jesus Christ and his salvation, which completes the hermeneutical unity and noetic understanding of the Bible.

> And he said to them, "Is a lamp brought in to be put under a basket, or under a bed, and not on a stand? For nothing is hidden except to be made manifest; nor is anything secret except to come to light. If anyone has ears to hear, let him hear." And he said to them, "Pay attention to what you hear: with the measure you use, it will be measured to you, and still more will be added to you. For

---

49. Hays, *Echoes of Scripture in the Gospels*, 188.
50. Burridge, *Four Gospels, One Jesus?*, 78.
51. Hays, *Echoes of Scripture in the Gospels*, 349.
52. Hays, *Echoes of Scripture in the Gospels*, 350.
53. Hays, *Echoes of Scripture in the Gospels*, 249.
54. Hays, *Echoes of Scripture in the Gospels*, 350.

to the one who has, more will be given, and from the one who has not, even what he has will be taken away." (Mark 4:21–5)

According to Hays, this passage teaches Mark's and Jesus' hermeneutical approach to understanding the Scriptures.[55] The call is to "measure generously in interpreting the word" because "still more rewards follow."[56] In other words, the call is to hear or integrate the scriptural echoes and concealed notes of Jesus Christ and his salvation in an Old Testament text. Failure to do so results in becoming a "stingy hearer who hears only the literal surface sense" and in "diminishing returns, leading finally to nothing but impoverishment."[57]

Therefore, Mark reads Scripture Christocentrically, but in an indirect and allusive manner, "giving just enough clues to tease the reader into further exploration and reflection."[58] Whereas Matthew reads Scripture openly by illuminating clear connections between the Old Testament and Jesus Christ and his salvation, Mark reads Scripture mysteriously by unearthing clues and artifacts in the Old Testament and then holds out a shovel for the reader to continue the excavation.

Read a Dramatic Scripture with Luke

Luke's voice is the dramatic storyteller. He unfolds the story of promise through Israel's history toward its fulfillment in the story of Jesus Christ. Per Hays, "Luke's hermeneutical strategy, then, is to re-narrate the story of Israel in such a way that the story of Jesus and the church can confidently be recognized as the fulfillment of the divine plan of salvation, for Israel and for the whole world."[59] Luke's extended citation of Isaiah 4:3–5 demonstrates his pattern of reading Israel's story as coming to a dramatic conclusion in Jesus Christ and his salvation.

> As it is written in the book of the words of Isaiah the prophet, "The voice of one crying in the wilderness: 'Prepare the way of the Lord, make his paths straight. Every valley shall be filled, and every mountain and hill shall be made low, and the crooked shall become straight, and the rough places shall become level ways, and all flesh shall see the salvation of God.'" (Luke 3:4–6)

---

55. Hays, *Echoes of Scripture in the Gospels*, 101.
56. Hays, *Echoes of Scripture in the Gospels*, 101.
57. Hays, *Echoes of Scripture in the Gospels*, 101.
58. Hays, *Echoes of Scripture in the Gospels*, 98.
59. Hays, *Echoes of Scripture in the Gospels*, 353.

The original historical meaning of Isaiah 4:3–5 is the announcement of the good news that Israel's exile is coming to an end by the victorious march of the Lord of Israel (Pole 1 of the Gospel Arc). Luke reads Isaiah 4:3–5 by integrating the original historical meaning with its ultimate meaning in Jesus Christ and his salvation (Pole 2). Therefore, Luke completes the meaning of Isaiah 4:3–5 in the revelatory arrival of Jesus Christ. As well, Jesus' arrival signals the end of Israel's exile, as the Lord of Israel who leads Israel victoriously out of exile in Isaiah is none other than the Lord Jesus Christ himself. For Luke, Jesus is the end of Israel's exile because the Lord himself has come to deliver God's people from the ultimate exile, to which the original historical exile always pointed. This example of Luke's narrative art inspired Hays' words:

> Luke is above all a storyteller ... the story he tells has the character of a dramatic epic ... sweeping in scope and measured in pace. The story's overall message finally emerges with lucidity, but Luke takes his time in allowing the plot to unfold on a grand scale.... Luke's narrative is symphonic. It develops long melody lines, plays variations upon them in multiple movements, but finally brings them all together as part of a unified artistic plan—a plan whose composer, Luke insists, is God.[60]

Read Scripture Backwards with John

John's voice is an explicit call to read backwards through the lens of Jesus Christ and his salvation to ultimately understand the Old Testament Scriptures (John 5:39–47). John sees the Old Testament Scriptures as containing divinely embedded signifiers that prefigure Jesus Christ and his salvation. These signifiers carry a surplus of meaning that only come to light retrospectively through the final revelatory lens of Jesus Christ and his salvation. John builds his hermeneutical case early by recording Philip's words to Nathanael: "We have found him of whom Moses in the Law and also the prophets wrote, Jesus of Nazareth, the son of Joseph" (John 1:45).

Why does John explicitly state and employ a retrospective hermeneutic for the Scriptures?[61] John's answer is hermeneutically cosmic. Jesus Christ is God incarnate (John 1:14), that is, the eternal "Word" of God (John 1:1–3). In other words, Jesus Christ is the ultimate eternal verbal action, speech act, or "Word" of God (John 1:1–3). Therefore, all the verbal actions

---

60. Hays, *Echoes of Scripture in the Gospels*, 275.
61. John 1:45; 5:39–47.

of God performed and recorded in redemptive history are inherently Christ-centered and laced with traces of Jesus Christ, the eternal Word of God. Hays explains John's *Logos* logic this way:

> All this works hermeneutically because, at the beginning and the end of the day, Jesus is the *Logos*, the Word present before creation. All creation breathes with *his* life. He is the divine Wisdom whose very being is the blueprint of all reality. For John the Evangelist, therefore, all of Israel's Scripture is a figural web woven with latent prefigurations of the One without whom not one thing came into being.[62]

Therefore, John understands the Old Testament Scriptures to be a "huge web of Christological signifiers generated by the pretemporal eternal logos as intimations of his truth and glory."[63] This means that although the "huge web of Christological signifiers" are present in the Old Testament Scriptures, they are not readily seen, understood, or embraced apart from the final revelatory light of Jesus Christ and his salvation (John 5:39–47). Reading backwards for John is not only hermeneutically logical because Jesus is the eternal Word of God, but it is also hermeneutically necessary because Jesus is the eternal Word of God become flesh.

Read Scripture with the Apostle Paul

The Apostle Paul not only decided to build his life and ministry around "Jesus Christ and him crucified," but also commends "Jesus Christ and him crucified" (1 Cor 2:2) as the only way to remove the hermeneutical and existential veil that covers every human heart. In 2 Corinthians 3, Paul asserts that the original historical meaning of the Old Testament is not enough around which to build a life, church, and ministry. In fact, if lives, churches, and ministries are restricted to the original historical teaching of the Old Testament alone, then a ministry of condemnation and death is perpetuated (2 Cor 3:9, 7).

THE HERMENEUTICAL VEIL

The hermeneutical veil is a textual blindness to the "eschatological glory" in the old covenant/Moses, which is Christ.[64] The Old Testament Scrip-

---

62. Hays, *Echoes of Scripture in the Gospels*, 344.
63. Hays, *Echoes of Scripture in the Gospels*, 343.
64. Barnett, *Second Epistle to the Corinthians*, 195.

tures (old covenant/Moses) are incomplete apart from Jesus Christ and his salvation (new covenant/the Spirit). Therefore, to treat the Old Testament Scriptures as complete revelation, as if the original historical meaning were enough to understand accurately and apply the Bible, is to perpetuate the hermeneutical veil: "For to this day, when they read the old covenant, that same veil remains unlifted, because only through Christ is it taken away (2 Cor 3:14)." Paul Barnett explains that Paul himself "sat in the synagogue Sabbath after

> Sabbath listening to the reading of the old covenant/Moses, but blinded to its glory, which pointed toward Christ. Moreover, as a Christian, he had preached Christ in the synagogues, explaining how the Scriptures (i.e., the Law and the Prophets—cf. Luke 24:44–46) had been fulfilled by the Messiah Jesus (Acts 13:15; 17:2–3), only to be faced with the obduracy of his hearers."[65]

Therefore, according to the Apostle Paul, reading the Old Testament Scriptures in light of the final and full revelation of Jesus Christ and his salvation is the only way to lift the hermeneutical veil—"only through Christ is it taken away" (2 Cor 3:14).

The Existential Veil

The existential veil is a metaphor for the spiritual blindness that "lies over [human] hearts" (2 Cor 3:15) and hardens minds (2 Cor 3:14) to Jesus Christ and his salvation. Biblically and theologically, the existential veil is part of original sin.

The hermeneutical veil points to mishandling the Bible by not integrating the Old Testament Scriptures to their ultimate climax in Jesus Christ and his salvation. The existential veil points to mishandling one's life by not understanding and relying upon Jesus Christ and his salvation. Therefore, in terms of functional Bible reading and communication, the existential veil contributes to the hermeneutical veil (2 Cor 3:14–16) by relying exclusively upon the Old Testament's original historical meaning.

Who Will Remove the Veil?

Who will deliver mankind from hermeneutical and existential blindness? The answer, according to the Apostle Paul, is the good news of hermeneutical and existential freedom in Jesus Christ: "But when one turns to the Lord,

---

65. Barnett, *Second Epistle to the Corinthians*, 193–4.

the veil is removed. Now the Lord is the Spirit, and where the Spirit of the Lord is, there is freedom" (2 Cor 3:16–17).[66]

Barnett explains, "Paul is saying, in effect, that only as Israelites turn to Christ, on the basis of the preaching of the gospel, will they discern the inner meaning and glory of the old covenant. Apart from Christ those who remain under that covenant remain veiled to the eschatological glory to which it pointed."[67]

Reading Scripture with the Apostle Paul means discovering the hermeneutical arc between the original historical meaning of an Old Testament passage (i.e., the old covenant/Moses) and the final and full revelatory meaning of Jesus Christ and his salvation (i.e., the new covenant/the Spirit). Every Old Testament passage can be integrated with or connected to the "surpassing glory" of the overall message of the Bible (2 Cor 3:10), the climax of God's revelation in Jesus Christ.

Every Old Testament passage or speech act reveals a facet of Jesus Christ and his salvation to reach and renew hearts. Building a life, church, and ministry only around the Old Testament's original historical meaning and intention is living under a hermeneutical and existential veil (2 Cor 3:7, 9). Building a life, church, and ministry around "Jesus Christ and him crucified" (1 Cor 2:2), however, is freedom. It is participating in personal and corporate gospel renewal or "being transformed into the same image from one degree of glory to another. For this comes from the Lord who is the Spirit" (2 Cor 3:17–18).

CONCLUSION

How did Jesus and the New Testament writers read the Bible? The answer is they read the Scriptures retrospectively through the final revelatory lens of Jesus Christ's life, death, and resurrection. The revelatory act of Jesus Christ and his resurrection changed everything, including how to read the Bible.

Therefore, there are now two historical revelatory poles to embrace when reading, applying, and communicating the Bible: Pole 1 is the textual pole of the original historical meaning of a given passage, and Pole 2 is the contextual pole of Jesus Christ and his salvation. The semantic force of meaning flows both ways between the poles. The original historical meaning of a given passage (Pole 1) gives a pattern of significance to Jesus Christ and his salvation (Pole 2). Jesus Christ and his salvation (Pole 2) involves,

---

66. Hermeneutical and existential justification is followed by ongoing hermeneutical and existential sanctification.

67. Barnett, *Second Epistle to the Corinthians*, 195.

fulfills, escalates, corresponds to, rereads, and completes all previous revelation in its historically partial or incomplete form (Pole 1). Therefore, a Gospel Arc is formed between the two poles.

One reads both forwards and backwards along the Gospel Arc—forward from the biblical text to Jesus Christ and his salvation by discovering and following the divinely embedded gospel threads in the text that give Jesus Christ and his salvation a pattern of significance; and backwards from Jesus Christ and his salvation to the biblical text by looking through the lens of the gospel in order to reread, reinterpret, or to map more meaning onto the original historical meaning. This Gospel Arc is the way the New Testament writers teach us to read, apply, and communicate the Bible.

In other words, the Bible requires a bi-directional reading: 1) to discover the original historical meaning of a text, and 2) to integrate the original historical meaning of the text into the ultimate revelatory message of the Bible, Jesus Christ, and his salvation. Therefore, as Hays explicates, Jesus and the New Testament writers are calling today's readers to

> retrain our sensibilities as readers and . . . reshape our perception of what is real. If we learn from them how to read, we will approach the reading of Scripture with a heightened awareness of story, metaphor, prefiguration, allusion, echo, reversal, and irony. To read Scripture well we must bid farewell to plodding literalism and rationalism in order to embrace a complex poetic sensibility. The Gospel writers are trying to teach us to become more interesting people—by teaching us to be more interesting readers.[68]

Taking Jesus with you to read the Bible changes everything.

---

68. Hayes, *Echoes of Scripture in the Gospels*, 360.

Chapter 14

The Power of Crafting a Sermon Message

LIVE A GOSPEL LIFE

A "Gospel Life"[1] is learning to build your messy life and relationships around Jesus and his salvation. The intelligent and mystical interaction we have with Jesus and his salvation by faith with the Bible changes us, our relationships, and the way we relate to everything.

This change is historically described as *gospel renewal*. Gospel-growth in people might be stickier for you. Gospel growth may be defined as *experiencing Jesus Christ and his salvation with the Bible by faith in a justifying and sanctifying way*. Experiencing gospel growth or renewal in all of life is learning to live a "Gospel Life." The two components that make up the phrase "gospel renewal" or "gospel growth" are critical to understand.

The "gospel" is Jesus and his salvation, his person and work. It is who Jesus is and what Jesus did *for* us, and therefore what he freely gives us. In other words, the gospel is the *Jesus-events* plus the *thick inscripturated messages* about those events. Therefore, Jesus' historical incarnation, life, death, resurrection, present reign, plus the interpenetrating interpretations of those Jesus-events (divine messages), collectively comprise the gospel.

---

1. "Gospel Life" comes from Keller, *Gospel in Life*.

The divine messages of the Jesus-events or the gospel come in a vast matrix of ideas and images throughout the redemptive history of the Bible. They provide a grammar for the gospel that is simultaneously distinct and inseparable in all its legal, dynamic, and eschatological aspects.

Therefore, there are no false choices between the history of salvation, order of salvation, and the apocalyptic aspects of salvation. Nor between the individual and the community, the personal and the cosmic, the legal and the dynamic, and the covenantal and the eschatological aspects of the salvation Jesus accomplished.[2] In other words, Jesus' salvation is comprehensive. It requires the vast grammar of the Bible to unleash its divine energies into our lives and the world (Rom 1:16).

The vast grammar of the gospel in all the Bible is good news or "news of victory"[3] of Jesus and what he has done—comprehensively. It is not good advice about what we do, nor is it the weird practice of turning one aspect of Jesus' salvation into a "my precious" that rules them all. "If we were to sum up the content of the Gospel in a single word, it would be Jesus the Christ."[4]

Furthermore, the good news message of Jesus Christ and his victorious work "does not merely declare salvation; it effects it . . . it is equated with its actuality."[5] The gospel establishes its own reality; it creates a whole new world. It reaches and renews lives, the home, relationships, the church, communities, places, cultures, and eventually heaven and earth itself. In other words, the gospel carries divine energies with it—divine life and power to change everything.[6] As we have said before, the gospel is *good news, not good advice.*

The personal renewal or growth that the gospel brings engages all the faculties of a united heart: 1) clarity to the mind, 2) realness to the heart, and

---

2. It is crucial to note the simultaneously distinct and inseparable aspects of Jesus' comprehensive salvation. Failure to do so inevitably ends in a self-imposed prison of false choices. For a helpful discussion of the apparent false choices imprisoning the church today, see Horton, *Justification*, 17–53. See also, Fleming Rutledge's helpful discussion of the varied aspects of Jesus' comprehensive salvation in *Crucifixion: Understanding the Death of Jesus Christ*, especially 207–13. Both Horton and Rutledge highlight the importance of avoiding one distinguishing central dogma that inevitably swallows up the other aspects of Jesus' comprehensive salvation.

3. "Euangelion," in *Theological Dictionary of the New Testament*, 722.

4. "Euangelion," in *Theological Dictionary of the New Testament*, 731.

5. "Euangelion," in *Theological Dictionary of the New Testament*, 7.

6. "The Gospel is not an empty word; it is effective power which brings to pass what it says because God is its author . . . The Gospel effects what it proclaims . . . it goes forth and works and produces fruit" (from "Euangelion," in *Theological Dictionary of the New Testament*, 731–33).

3) inclination of the will beyond new or true information. Experiencing Jesus and his salvation by faith looks like: 1) a new experience of Jesus Christ and his salvation by faith that is justifying, and 2) a deepening and maturing experience of Jesus Christ and his salvation by faith that is sanctifying. Thus, the Christian life is a life of constant renewal or gospel growth—of rediscovery of the gospel.

The renewal that the gospel brings also takes place immediately on two levels—the personal and the corporate (the church). Just as we are being renewed individually through encounters with Jesus and his salvation in the Bible, so too are relationships and communities of people being reached with this same renewal.

In the context of preaching, corporate renewal occurs when preachers and hearers experience Jesus and his salvation with the biblical text by faith while it is being preached. Therefore, gospel renewal with the Bible reaches and renews not only individual lives but also the home, relationships, the church, places, communities, and cultures—and one day everything.

DO GOSPEL MINISTRY

It is easy in pastoral ministry today to be about anything and everything but Jesus Christ and his salvation. It is a pastoral hazard to build a life and ministry around good things that functionally become pseudo-saviors and yet are unable to carry the weight of savior-hood. Only the grace of God revealed and released in Jesus Christ and his salvation can reach and renew lives, the home, pastors, the church, communities, and the surrounding culture.

According to the Apostle Paul, nothing can replace Jesus Christ and his salvation to save comprehensively, both in terms of justification and sanctification: "for I decided to know nothing among you except Jesus Christ and him crucified" (1 Cor 2:2). Gospel growth or experiencing Jesus and his salvation by faith is both the practice and power of the Apostle Paul's ministry.

The Gospel as a Way to See Ministry

The Apostle Paul's statement in 1 Corinthians 2:2 communicates an apostolic vision or philosophy of ministry both in terms of what it says and what it does not say. Building a pastoral ministry around nothing except Jesus Christ and his salvation is remarkable, since it was Paul's approach to minister to both the skeptic and the Christian. In other words, the message of

Jesus Christ and his salvation is not only how Paul first reached or evangelized the Corinthians, but also how he continued to renew or sanctify them.

What is it about "nothing but Jesus" that is so transformative in ministry in terms of justification and sanctification, or in terms of reaching and renewing the un-churched and the churched? The answer is the verbal power of "him crucified," as opposed to "him exemplified."

The Apostle's governing ministry vision was Jesus Christ as Savior, not merely moral example, spiritual leader, gifted teacher, ministry activist, or miracle worker. According to Paul, only the verbal power of Jesus Christ as Savior reaches and renews both the skeptic and the Christian. Therefore, the ultimate apostolic aim for all ministry is to experience Jesus and his salvation by faith or gospel growth in all of life.

The Gospel as a Way to Communicate the Bible

The Apostle Paul's statement in 1 Corinthians 2:2 concerning pastoral ministry being built around nothing except Jesus Christ and his salvation is also remarkable given the fact that the only Bible the Apostle had was the Old Testament. Nowhere in the Old Testament is "Jesus Christ and him crucified" explicitly mentioned. This means, in Keller's words, that "Paul understood that all Scripture ultimately pointed to Jesus and his salvation; that every prophet, priest, and king was shedding light on the ultimate Prophet, Priest, and King. To present the Bible 'in its fullness' was to preach Christ as the main theme and substance of the Bible's message."[7]

Paul's Christocentric understanding of the Old Testament was why he wrote in 1 Corinthians 15:3-4, "Christ died for our sins *in accordance with the Scriptures*, that he was buried, that he was raised on the third day *in accordance with the Scriptures*." Jesus Christ and his salvation *is* in accordance with the Old Testament Scriptures. Therefore, according to the Apostle Paul, experiencing Jesus and his salvation by faith or gospel renewal is the fundamental aim of all the Scriptures, both the Old and New Testament.

The Gospel as a Way to Practice Pastoral Care

Finally, the Apostle Paul's statement in 1 Corinthians 2:2 concerning pastoral ministry being built around nothing except Jesus Christ and his salvation is remarkable given its scope for the human condition or people's lives. The Apostle decided to know nothing but Jesus Christ and him crucified as

---

7. Keller, *Preaching: Communicating Faith in an Age of Skepticism*, 15.

the solution to address the Corinthian church's well-documented range of personal, interpersonal, and corporate problems.

Therefore, according to Paul, experiencing Jesus and his salvation by faith or gospel renewal is sufficient to address the multiform needs and manifestations of the broken human condition.[8] Taking Jesus with you to address the complexities of the human condition provides the best kind of spiritual resources for pastoral care.

CONCLUSION

The Apostle Paul decided to build his life and ministry around the good news of Jesus Christ and his salvation because the gospel message is Jesus and his power to save comprehensively. All of Paul's personal and ministerial confidence hung on a gospel message that releases the personal active presence of Jesus Christ into people's lives, relationships, and the world (Rom 1:16), thereby producing justifying and sanctifying faith-on-the-spot or gospel renewal.

Paul was convinced that the message of Jesus and his salvation in all of Scripture comprises living and active words. It has verbal power—it produces personal and corporate gospel renewal; it does the work of ministry. Therefore, Paul boldly proclaims the gospel as the personal active presence of Jesus and his salvation in the world, "Of this you have heard before in the word of truth, the gospel, which has come to you, as indeed in the whole world it is bearing fruit and growing—as it also does among you, since the day you heard it and understood the grace of God in truth" (Col 1:5–6). The gospel has a course of its own.

Therefore, according to the Apostle, experiencing Jesus and his salvation by faith is the pattern of the Holy Spirit's work in a community. There is a need for preaching that aligns itself with the pattern of the Holy Spirit's work in a community, that is, to experience Jesus with the Bible. Taking Jesus with you in preaching changes everything.

---

8. Patrick Lencioni in his bestselling book *Advantage: Why Organizational Health Trumps Everything Else in Business*, 8, points to personal and organizational health or renewal as the single most important factor in the business world: "I've become absolutely convinced that the seminal difference between successful companies and mediocre or unsuccessful ones has little, if anything, to do with what they know or how smart they are; it has everything to do with how healthy they are."

Appendix A

The Gospel Arc Preaching Manual

Round 1: Listen to the Text

Pole 1
*The Original Historical Meaning

Pole 2
*The Ultimate Overall Meaning of all Scripture (Jesus Christ and His Salvation)

The Gospel Arc

LISTEN TO THE TEXT

1. Listen for Yourself (become an "intelligent mystic"):

2. Listen to the World of the Text (enter into the life of the text—its sights, sounds, and scents . . . the world of the text must come before our ideas about it . . . the world of the text must be allowed to shape our ideas rather than vice-versa):

3. Listen for Others (become a "physician of the soul"):

APPENDIX A

Listening Tool:

- Listen to God in and with the text
- Luxuriate in the text
- Slow, gentle reading
- A spontaneous, even naïve engagement with the text
- Learning to listen, think, feel, see, imagine, encounter, and ask questions of the text in the tpresence of God
- Imagination and empathy come first, and analysis comes second
- The Bible is a "stranger thing", admit it and be curious

Round 2: Understand the Text

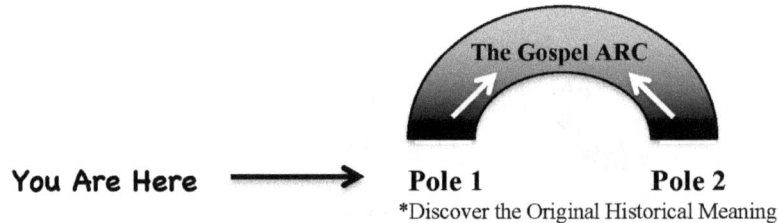

The Gospel Arc

UNDERSTAND THE TEXT

1. Create a *Textual Map* (itemize main and supporting ideas):
2. Write a *Running Commentary* (answer significant questions in the text—literary, historical, theological . . . employ study aids after some sweat equity in the text):

Interpretive Tool (pay special attention to significant):

- Words

- Ideas
- Images
- Repetitions
- Connector words
- Allusions and quotes from other places in the Bible
- Characters and dialogue
- Scenes and places
- Actions and events
- Historical background
- The unexpected, unusual surprises, out of place details, and questions that provoke you in the text (great place for the deepest meaning to hide)

Round 3: Discover the Text's Message

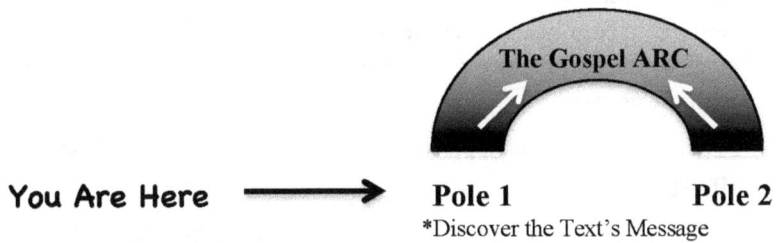

The Gospel Arc

DISCOVER THE TEXT'S MESSAGE

1. Identify a particular aspect of the *Human Condition* (HC) addressed in the text.

Human Condition Tool (record in a sticky statement or vivid image):

- What is the *God-sized* or *God-shaped* "hole" found in the text due to the functional impact of the absence of God upon the human condition (i.e. the fallen condition is both deprived and depraved)?
- What is the *"mental map"* (way of seeing) and/or *"heart map"* (way of trusting) of the individual people and/or corporate people (culture) in the text?
- What is the universal human need, burden, condition, or conflict in or behind the text?
- Who are the *people* or what are the *places* in view in the text?
- What is the universal human condition of the participants and/or hearers being addressed?
- What required the writing of this text?
- Why might the Holy Spirit have inspired the text?
- What is the universal human need, burden, condition, or conflict in the text that requires the grace of Jesus Christ and his salvation?
- What are the *background beliefs* or *alternate beliefs* in the text that correspond to your hearers in order to *connect* (point of contact) and *challenge* (push on pressure point) and ultimately *re-connect* (re-enchant with the gospel)?
- What is the *idol*, god-replacement, substitute-savior, or self-salvation strategy in the text?

2. Identify the Primary Thing the Text is *Saying* or the *Big Idea* of the Text.

Big Idea Tool (record in a sticky statement or vivid image):

- What is the primary powerful thing the text is *saying*?
- What is the dominant thought, idea, image, story, need, "Aha!," subject, theme, or content in the text?
- What is the "freshly squeezed" essence of the text?
- This text is about _____.
- The "Speech" in Speech-Act.

3. Identify the primary thing the text is *doing* with what it is saying or the *Applied Big Idea* of the text. Because God's Word *does* what it *says*!

Applied Big Idea Tool (record in a sticky statement or vivid image):

- What is the primary powerful thing the text is *doing* with what it is saying?
- Where is the passage *going*?
- Where is the passage *taking us*?
- What is the *"so what?,"* force, function, movement, intention, action, practical difference, or transformative possibility of the controlling content?
- This text is doing _____.
- What are the energies being imparted by the text?
- The "Act" in Speech-Act.
- How the gospel re-enchants lives, relationships, communities, places, all of life (the world).

Literary Tool:

- If the text is *narrative literature* or a *story*, then discover how the setting, characters, conflict or plot line, and resolution or lack thereof communicate the three interpretive textual tracks (i.e., the human condition, Big Idea, and Applied Big Idea of the text).
- If the text is *propositional literature* or a *logical argument*, then discover how the flow of the main and supporting ideas communicate the three interpretive textual tracks.
- If the text is *law* or an *ethical principle*, then discover how the ideal or anti-ideal communicate the three interpretive textual tracks.
- If the text is *wisdom literature*, then discover how the *fabric of creation* (i.e. the regular patterns or order in creation) or the *futility of creation* (i.e. the irregular patterns or active de-creation because of sin in creation) communicates the three interpretive textual tracks.

- If the text is *poetic literature*, then discover how the image that brings the *world of ideas* and the the *world of experience* together communicates the three interpretive textual tracks.
- If the text is *apocalyptic literature*, then discover how the visual revelation (rather than aural) communicates the three interpretive textual tracks.

Round 4: Discover the Textual Jesus

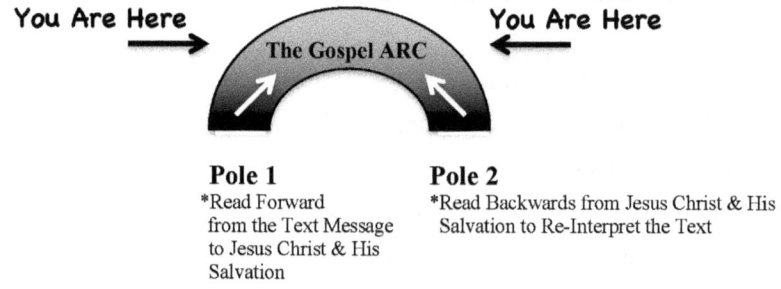

The Gospel Arc

DISCOVER THE TEXTUAL JESUS

1. *Read forward* by following the divinely embedded *Gospel Threads* in the text. These threads carry a *surplus of meaning* (think it out below).

Gospel Thread Tool (Pole 1 gives a *pattern of significance* to Jesus Christ and his salvation):

- An *attribute* and/or *action of God* in the text that is addressing the universal human condition, need, or burden in the text. Follow this gospel thread to its ultimate example or embodiment in Jesus Christ and his salvation.
- A *theme* or *idea* in the text. Follow this gospel thread to its ultimate resolution in Jesus Christ and his salvation.

APPENDIX A   153

- A *law* or *biblical ethic* in the text. Follow this gospel thread to its completion in Jesus Christ and his salvation.
- An *image* in the text. Follow this gospel thread to its ultimate target in Jesus Christ and his salvation.
- A *type* or *pattern* in the text. Follow this gospel thread to its ultimate fulfillment, substance, or perfection in Jesus Christ and his salvation.
- A *story of an individual or community* in the text. Follow this gospel thread to its ultimate bigger story of Jesus Christ and his salvation.
- An *instinct* or *sense* in the text. Follow this gospel thread to its ultimate convergence on Jesus Christ and his salvation.
- A *sin and its consequences*, a *heart and life issue*, a *cultural heart and life issue*, a *spiritual need*, a *universal human "hole," condition, burden, and problem* in the text. Follow these gospel threads to their ultimate solution in Jesus Christ and his salvation.
- The *human longing in the text*. Follow this gospel thread to its ultimate satisfaction in JesusChrist and his salvation.
- The *functional human trust*, hope, love, worship, salvation, justification, or God-replacement in the text. Follow this gospel thread to its ultimate source and satisfaction in Jesus Christ and his salvation.
- The *grace at work in the text*. Follow this gospel thread to its ultimate source in Jesus Christ and his salvation.

2. *Read backwards* by looking through the *Gospel Lens* to re-interpret or find the *surplus of meaning* in the text (think it out below).

Gospel Lens Tool (Pole 2 *maps more meaning* onto, completes, or reinterprets Pole 1):

Look at how Jesus and his salvation:

- Address the universal human need, condition, or burden in the text.
- Address what the text is *saying* (i.e. the ultimate Big Idea of the text).
- Accomplish what the text is *doing* (i.e. the ultimate Applied Big Idea of the text).
- Solve tensions in the text.
- Involve, correspond to, map more meaning onto, fulfill, escalate, or complete the signifiers (gospel threads) in the text.

- Interpret the Old Testament allusions, echoes, or quotations in the New Testament text.
- Provide the source or ultimate work of grace in the text.

3. Craft the specific *Textual Jesus* in the text into *one* sticky statement or vivid image (this freshly crafted *Textual Jesus* is what the sermon is built around):

Textual Jesus Tool:

- Connect Pole 1 and Pole 2 to each other to form a Gospel Arc. This is your *Textual Jesus*.
- Take 2 lumps of clay (Pole 1 and Pole 2) and craft ONE specific aspect of Jesus Christ and his salvation from the text.
- What is a specific aspect of Jesus Christ and his salvation in the text to reach and renew lives, relationships, places, the world?
- Locate the Jesus of the text or the Word in the Word.

Round 5: Craft a Sermon Message

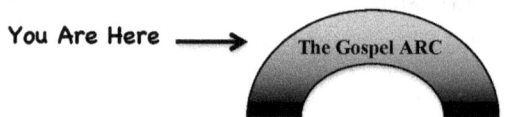

*Build the Sermon Around the *Textual Jesus*
**A Gospel ARC Sermon is Built Around Re-Presenting Jesus Christ & His Salvation according to the Particular Way of the Text in a Way that is Clear to the Mind and Real to the Heart

The Gospel Arc

CRAFT A SERMON MESSAGE

1. The sermon should say and do *one powerful thing* not many things. Therefore, craft a *Sermon Message*. Pick a point!

APPENDIX A   155

Sermon Message Tool 1:

First, a sermon message is crafted around the five interpretive tracks below:
1. Your recorded sticky statement or vivid image for the *universal human and/or cultural condition* being specifically addressed in the text.
2. Your recorded sticky statement or vivid image for the text's *Big Idea* (or the primary thing the passage is saying).
3. Your recorded sticky statement or vivid image for the text's *Applied Big Idea* (or the primary thing the passage is doing with what it is saying).
4. Your recorded sticky statement or vivid image for the *universal human and/or cultural condition* being specifically addressed in the text.
5. Your recorded sticky statement or vivid image for the *Textual Jesus* (or the specific aspect of Jesus Christ and his salvation revealed in the text).
6. The specific human and/or cultural need of *contemporary hearers* (the local listening need).

Sermon Message Tool 2:

Second, there are three preferred ways to craft a Sermon Message around the five interpretive tracks above:
1. *Blend them all together* into one *sticky statement, vivid image,* or *suspenseful question*. Whether blended together into one sticky statement, vivid image, or suspenseful question, the individual tracks become the supporting ideas or movements of the Sermon Map.
    Sticky Statement:
    Vivid Image:
    or Suspenseful Question:

2. *Lead with one track while the other tracks stand off stage* waiting to make key appearances during the event of the sermon. In other words, the lead track rules them all by becoming the Sermon Message and the other tracks play key supporting roles as needed in the Sermon Map.
    Lead Track:
    Supporting Track(s):

3. *Follow a narrative form* that places the individual tracks into the plot line of one ultimate over-arching story or Sermon Message. In other

words, "This is a story about ___." What you fill in is your Sermon Message. How you tell the story is your Sermon Map.

This is a story about _____." This is your Sermon Message:
Tell the story with the individual Interpretive Tracks (Sermon Map):

2. Once you have *Crafted a Sermon Message*, build everything around it. *Build A Sermon Map* in oral form (natural scripting to be heard not read). Keep in mind:

- The aim of preaching is to experience Jesus Christ and his salvation with the text in order to reach and renew lives, the home, relationships, the church, places, communities, and the surrounding culture.
- In other words, the aim of preaching is gospel-growth in people.
- Therefore, the Sermon Map should best support this aim.

Appendix B

A Sample Week with the Gospel Arc Preaching Manual

GUIDELINES:

1. This is an *ideal*—if it just weren't for the people who get in the way (ha!), your own heart, or an uncooperative text.
2. This is a *learned* schedule—use it to help discover your own.
3. Do as much outside reading as possible to help prepare you, to fuel creativity, and to find supporting material.

Tuesday—Friday	
Listen to the Text	(Round 1 = 1 hour)
Understand the Text	(Round 2 = 1 hour)
Discover the Text's Message	(Round 3 = 1 hour)
Discover the Gospel Arc	(Round 4 = 1 hour)
Craft a Sermon Message	(Round 5a = 1 hour)
Build a Sermon Map	(Round 5b = 1 hour)
	Total 6 hours

Saturday	Sunday
Prepare Myself (1 hour)	Prepare Myself (1 hour)
Edit Sermon Map (i.e., for "Orality" or for the hearer (2–3 hours)	Final Internalization of Sermon Map—mark it all up with pen and colored highlighters (1 hour)
Total 3–4 hours	Total 2 hours

Prep Time versus Sermon Length	
Range for Weekly Prep Time	10–20 hours
Range for Sermon Length	25–35 minutes

Appendix C

A Sermon Transcript of Romans 10:1–4: "The Deeper Struggle"

Have you heard the story about the Calvinist who falls down the stairs? Sure, you have. After his tumble, he brushes himself off and says, "Man, I'm glad *that's* over!" Well, we can't say *that* yet, can we?

The Pandemic isn't over—yet. Racial tensions aren't over—yet. Riots aren't over—yet. Political power plays aren't over—yet. The culture war isn't over—yet. Intensified violence in urban areas aren't over—yet. The confusion and chaos over "Whose Justice?" isn't over—yet. Even in the Church. Is it Marxist justice, race-identity justice, nihilistic justice, liberal justice, conservative justice, fascist justice, humanistic justice, American justice, Chinese justice? Whose justice is it?

Verse 2 in today's text says, "For I bear them witness that they have a zeal for God, but not according to knowledge (or "but not according to truth or reality"). "Zeal" means "intense passion," "intense commitment," "intense dedication." Paul is saying, "Listen, the people I'm talking about are *on fire*! On fire for God, his Law, justice, and righteousness!" But don't miss this. Paul is also saying, "But this is not a good thing."

Why is zeal without knowledge (truth, reality) not a good thing? The answer is because it's fanaticism, radicalism, extremism. Craziness. Just ask Paul. He dragged Christians out of their homes. Bullied them, beat them, stoned them, murdered them, terrorized them, took their stuff. Saul-Paul believed he was a "Blues Brother," that is, on a mission from God..

Zeal without knowledge (truth, reality) is everywhere. This is why a whole country could unite around the murder of George Floyd, and then splinter so quickly.

Zeal without knowledge (truth, reality) is why five-year-old Cannon Hinnant was innocently riding his bicycle in front of his house this past week, and someone (apparently motivated by racial hatred) walked up to him and shot him point blank in the head. Execution style. A five-year-old boy. And no one blinks an eye! No protests. No outrage. Nothing. Selective outrage is zeal without knowledge (truth, reality).

Zeal without knowledge (truth, reality) is why we are losing our minds on social media. And lost some friends because we are losing our minds on social media. It's why we've stopped talking to some family members and church friends.

Zeal without knowledge (truth, reality) is why the church is losing its mind. "Whose justice?" We use to know the answer to that. "God's justice!" we use to say. Now (either formally or functionally) we seem to promote a race-identity justice, that is, we are defining ourselves and others by the color of their skin. Which of course is salvation-by-race and its corresponding condemnation-by-race. It is seeing the world through the lens of race—everything is about race. It is treating others according to race—everything is a race ethic. It is slavery to the idol of race—everything for the god of race. Therefore, race-identity is its own alternative religion, doctrine, ethic, mission, kingdom, and church to Christianity. It is a false gospel.

So, *what* do we *do* when we're all crazy? Please stand for the reading of God's Word. Romans 10.1–4. Pray.

What do we do when we're all crazy?

Paul says, "First, don't be stupid about what's going on! Look at verse 3: "For, being ignorant of the righteousness of God, and seeking to establish their own, they did not submit to God's righteousness."

Don't be stupid about what? The answer is the deeper struggle. There's a deeper struggle than the Pandemic. There's a deeper struggle than the riots, shut-downs, upheaval, chaos, and all the multi-forms of fear trying to swallow us up. There's a deeper struggle than the political power plays of progressives and conservatives. There's a deeper struggle than the culture war playing out on high definition each evening. There's even a deeper struggle than zeal for God and justice—whatever that means. Paul is saying, "Don't be stupid about the deeper struggle."

What is the deeper struggle? The struggle for *righteousness*—"For, being ignorant of the righteousness of God, and seeking to establish their own, they did not submit to God's righteousness" (verse 3). The Struggle for Righteousness is the deepest struggle in the cosmos. It's the deepest struggle in your heart right now. It's the deepest struggle in your relationships—the source of most relational heartache and hardship. It's the deepest struggle behind addictions, obsessions, damaging behavior, abusive relationships, and racism. It's the deepest struggle in the home, church, workplace, as well as our communities, cities, and culture. It's the deepest struggle in racial tensions, political power plays, and destructive institutions and systems.

The Struggle for Righteousness is why David Zahl in his latest book, *Seculosity*, says, "If you want to understand what makes someone tick, or why they're behaving the way they are, trace the righteousness in play, and things will likely become clear . . . The longing for some form of righteousness is. . .the foundation of what it means to be human."

The Struggle for Righteousness is why Jonathan Haidt (a leading Psychologist) at the end of his research (now turned book titled, *The Righteous Mind*) says, "An obsession with righteousness. . .is the normal human condition."

The Struggle for Righteousness is why the great poet (T. S. Eliot) poetically penned:

Half the harm that is done in this world
Is due to people who want to feel important
They don't mean to do harm—but the harm does not interest them
Or they do not see it, or they justify it
Because they are absorbed in the endless struggle
To think well of themselves.

The Struggle for Righteousness is why life feels like a never-ending trial of measurements, judgments, pressure, stress, striving, exhaustion, anxiety, depression, and self-consciousness. The Struggle for Righteousness is why someone asked me this past week, "Why do I so desperately need to be recognized? It drives everything I do." By the way we usually don't see this in ourselves until we are NOT recognized! The Struggle for Righteousness is why we are idiots on Social Media. The Struggle for Righteousness is why accusation and condemnation are everywhere right now—the very air we all breathe. Think about it. If "righteousness" is now having the right views, beliefs, ideology, propaganda, lens, political persuasion, historical interpretation of the past, and/or the right race, culture, group, class, history, and power. . . . Then those who don't are accused and condemned. A world of accusation and condemnation is playing in the Evil One's backyard. Theologian Reinhold Neibuhr wrote, "there is no deeper pathos in the spiritual life of man than the cruelty of righteous people." Don't be stupid about the deeper struggle for righteousness. . . .

Zeal without knowledge (truth . . . reality) is everywhere today. What do we do when we're all crazy? First, don't be stupid about the deeper struggle for righteousness. Second, *end* your struggle for righteousness, and help others do the same.

Look at verse 4, "For Christ is the end of the law for righteousness to everyone who believes." Jesus *ends* the deep Struggle for Righteousness.

How? By giving you *his*! Look at the last phrase in verse 3 (literal translation): "they did not submit to the righteousness *from God*." From God! From God! From God! There is no righteousness *from us*. From our race, culture, color of our eyes, height, beauty, ideology, views, political positions, social activism (whether its peaceful or violent), virtue signaling on social media, effort to be a just person and non-racist. There is no righteousness *from us*. Period.

Look at the last phrase in verse 3 again (literal translation): "they did not submit to the righteousness *from God*." The use of "submit" is forceful. Intense. It points beyond us. It stirs up images of bending and bowing. Bending before a power beyond your powers. Bowing before a greatness way beyond you. Paul is saying that the "righteousness from God" is beyond you and your righteous powers. It is a righteousness from God himself—his very righteousness—that can only be received never achieved. In other words, only the "righteousness from God" (only a received-righteousness, only a grace-righteousness, only a Jesus-righteousness) is powerful enough to *end* your struggle for righteousness—in whatever form it comes in.

A Jesus-righteousness (the righteousness from God) is all the righteousness you need. End your struggle for righteousness. End your struggle to achieve righteousness. End your struggle to establish a righteousness of your own. End your struggle by the only power able to do it, a Jesus-righteousness. The superior righteousness of Another. Jesus is all the righteousness you need.

You are now free to not be defined by (find your identity in) your race, culture, color of your eyes, beauty, performance, work, wealth, your level of privilege (whatever that means!). You are now free to not define others (accept or condemn others) by their race, culture, level of privilege, views, failures, sins, preferences.

You are now free to disagree with someone and still be friends. You are now free to protest (or not). To be a cop (or not). To be wrong (or not). To stop being a jerk, bully, coward, self-important (or not! Ha!). You are free to love everyone back to life again. To make friends and have gospel conversations with everyone.

Your struggle for righteousness is over. You have all the righteousness you need. Jesus is all the righteousness you need.

Look at verse 1: "Brothers, my heart's desire and prayer to God for them is that they may be saved." Because Jesus is all the righteousness you need, you are now free to help others *end* their struggle for righteousness too.

Bibliography

Barnett, Paul. *The Second Epistle to the Corinthians*. The New International Commentary on The New Testament. Grand Rapids: Eerdmans, 1997.
Bayer, Oswald. *Martin Luther's Theology: A Contemporary Interpretation*. Grand Rapids: Eerdmans, 2008.
Bauckham, Richard. "Reading Scripture as a Coherent Story." In *The Art of Reading Scripture*, edited by Ellen F. Davis and Richard B. Hays, 38–53. Grand Rapids: Eerdmans, 2003.
Beale, G. K., ed. *The Right Doctrine from the Wrong Texts? Essays on the Use of the Old Testament in the New*. Grand Rapids: Baker, 1994.
Bruner, Frederick Dale. *A Matthew Commentary: The Christbook Matthew 1–12*. Grand Rapids: Eerdmans, 2004.
Burridge, Richard A. *Four Gospels, One Jesus? A Symbolic Reading*. 3rd ed. Grand Rapids: Eerdmans, 2014.
Chapell, Bryan. *Christ-Centered Preaching: Redeeming the Expository Sermon*. 2nd ed. Grand Rapids: Baker Academic, 2005.
Craddock, Fred. *Preaching*. Nashville: Abingdon, 1985.
Edwards, James. *The Gospel According to Luke*. The Pillar New Testament Commentary. Grand Rapids: Eerdmans, 2015.
France, R. T. *Jesus and the Old Testament*. Vancouver: Regent College Publishing, 1998.
Frei, Hans W. *The Eclipse of Biblical Narrative: A Study in Eighteenth and Nineteenth Century Hermeneutics*. New Haven: Yale University Press, 1974.
Goldsworthy, Graeme. *Preaching the Whole Bible as Christian Scripture: The Application of Biblical Theology to Expository Preaching*. Grand Rapids: Eerdmans, 2000.
Goldsworthy, Graeme. *Gospel-Centered Hermeneutics: Foundations and Principles of Evangelical Biblical Interpretation*. Downers Grove: IVP Academic, 2006.
Greidanus, Sidney. *Preaching Christ from the Old Testament*. Grand Rapids: Eerdmans, 1999.
———. *Sola Scriptura: Problems and Principles in Preaching Historical Texts*. Toronto: Wedge, 1970.
Hays, Richard B. *Echoes of Scripture in the Gospels*. Waco: Baylor University Press, 2016.
———. *Reading Backwards: Figural Christology and the Fourfold Gospel Witness*. Waco: Baylor University Press, 2014.

BIBLIOGRAPHY

Horton, Michael. *Justification*. New Studies in Dogmatics. 2 vols. Edited by Michael Horton et al. Grand Rapids: Zondervan, 2018.

Keller, Timothy. *Center Church: Doing Balanced, Gospel-Centered Ministry in Your City*. Grand Rapids: Zondervan, 2012.

———. *Hidden Christmas: The Surprising Truth Behind the Birth of Christ*. New York: Viking, 2016.

———. *Prayer: Experiencing Awe and Intimacy with God*. New York: Dutton, 2014.

———. *Preaching: Communicating Faith in an Age of Skepticism*. New York: Viking, 2015.

Keller, Timothy, and Edmund Clowney. "Preaching Christ in a Postmodern World." Lecture, Reformed Theological Seminary, Jackson, MS, Special Seminar on Christ and Culture. Accessed July 10, 2016.

Kittel, Gerhard, and Gerhard Friedrich, eds. *Theological Dictionary of the New Testament*. 10 vols. Translated and edited by Geoffrey W. Bromiley. Grand Rapids: Eerdmans, 1964.

Kuruvilla, Abraham. *Privilege the Text! A Theological Hermeneutic for Preaching*. Chicago: Moody, 2013.

Large, Alex. *The Mockingbird Devotional: Good News for Today (and Every Day)*. Edited by Ethan Richardson and Sean Norris. Charlottesville: Mockingbird Ministries, 2013.

Leithart, Peter J. *Deep Exegesis: The Mystery of Reading Scripture*. Waco: Baylor University Press, 2009.

Lencioni, Patrick. *The Advantage: Why Organizational Health Trumps Everything Else in Business*. San Francisco: Jossey-Bass, 2012.

Lindbeck, George. *The Church in a Postliberal Age*. Edited by James J. Buckley. Grand Rapids: Eerdmans, 2002.

Lloyd-Jones, Marytn. "Glorious Gospel; Glorious God: 1 Corinthians 15:1–4." Sermon, MLJ Trust. Accessed October 15, 2016. https://www.mljtrust.org/sermons-online/1-corinthians-15-1-4/glorious-gospel-glorious-god/.

Long, Thomas. *The Witness of Preaching*. 2nd ed. Louisville: Westminster John Knox, 2005.

Lovelace, Richard. *Dynamics of Spiritual Life: An Evangelical Theology of Renewal*. Downers Grove: Intervarsity Press, 1979.

Luther, Martin. *Commentary on Galatians*. Edited by John Prince Fallows. Grand Rapids: Kregel, 1979.

McKnight, Scot. *The King Jesus Gospel: The Original Good News Revisited*. Grand Rapids: Zondervan, 2011.

Moberly, R. W. L. *Bible, Theology, and Faith: A Study of Abraham and Jesus*. Cambridge Studies in Christian Doctrine. Cambridge: Cambridge University Press, 2000.

Millar, Gary, and Phil Campbell. *Saving Eutychus: How to Preach God's Word and Keep People Awake*. Kingsford: Matthias Media, 2013.

Motyer, Alec. *Preaching? Simple Teaching on Simply Preaching*. Geanies House, Fearn, Ross-shire: Christian Focus, 2013.

Murray, John. *Redemption: Accomplished and Applied*. Grand Rapids: Eerdmans, 1955.

Osbourne, Grant R. *Exegetical Commentary on the New Testament: Matthew*. Edited by Clinton E. Arnold. Grand Rapids: Zondervan, 2010.

Perkins, William. *The Art of Prophesying*. Rev. ed. Carlisle: The Banner of Truth Trust, 1996, 2011.

Rutledge, Fleming. *The Crucifixion: Understanding the Death of Jesus Christ.* Grand Rapids: Eerdmans, 2015.
Sertin, Johnny. "Sharing the Kingdom." Truett Theological Seminary discussion, London, May 20, 2016.
The Westminster Standards. *The Westminster Confession of Faith, The Larger Catechism, The Shorter Catechism.* Suwanee: Great Commission, 2007.
Thiselton, Anthony. *New Horizons in Hermeneutics: The Theory and Practice of Transforming Biblical Reading.* Grand Rapids: Zondervan, 1992.
Vanhoozer, Kevin. *Is There Meaning in the Text?* Grand Rapids: Zondervan, 1998.
Vitello, Paul. "Taking a Break from the Lord's Work." *The New York Times*, August 1, 2010.
Vos, Geerhardus. *Biblical Theology: Old and New Testaments.* Edinburgh: Banner of Truth Trust, 1996.
Ward, Timothy. *Words of Life: Scripture Is the Living and Active Word of God.* Downers Grove: IVP Academic, 2009.
Zahl, David. *Seculosity: How Career, Parenting, Technology, Food, Politics, and Romance Became Our New Religion and What to Do About It.* Minneapolis: Fortress, 2019.

Subject Index

acceptance
  before God, 19, 21
activate
  God, 9, 10, 12, 23, 46, 138, 156, 175
applying
  the gospel, 183
  the law, 183
author
  absent, 186
  divine, 198
  divine only, 117, 186, 188
  double view, 190, 192, 193, 195, 197, 198
  human, 188, 190, 193, 195, 198
  human only, 117, 186, 188, 190, 195
  inspired human, 117, 186, 188, 190, 195
  lonely, 188
  meaningful, 50, 116, 192

Bible
  being true, 9
  faith with, 12, 217
biblical
  criticism, 38
  principle, 27, 34, 200
  principles, 10, 12, 17, 36, 46, 145, 180
big idea
  applied, 61, 63, 66, 67, 95, 100, 101, 103, 105, 110, 119, 125, 129, 133, 135, 136, 139, 227, 229, 231
  of the text, 61, 226
  tool, 61, 94, 95, 226, 227

Christian
  life and ministry, 9
communion
  with God, 75, 145
condemnation
  functional, 21
  hostile powers of, 92, 148
corpse
  Adamic, 41
cross, 25, 103, 113, 114, 121, 135, 148, 178, 183

deliverance
  Jesus, 23
divine
  intrusion, 19

Edwards, James, 200
Enlightenment, 38, 168
  offspring of, 38
event
  divine, 138, 139

failure
  interpretive, 205

faith
  alone, 23, 83, 154, 157, 174, 175
  plus something, 23, 152
flesh
  of the, 29, 170, 178
  sinful, 170

Galatians, 31, 98, 152, 153, 154, 159, 175, 176
ghost writer, 188
glorification, 29, 149, 158, 171, 173
good advice
  addiction to, 34
good news
  not good advice, 14, 40, 54, 219
  of Jesus Christ, 13, 168, 222
gospel
  activates sanctification, 31
  grammar of, 12, 14, 219
  growth, 75, 135, 138, 160, 217, 220, 221
  is substitution, 171
  lens, 42, 117, 119, 120, 121, 123, 124, 125, 126, 127, 197, 204
  life, 217
  re-enchantment, 101
  renewal, 25, 31, 33, 52, 54, 56, 75, 164, 168, 215, 217, 220, 221, 222
  revolution, 12, 14
  self-activating, 11
  that which freely gives, 171
  threads, 65, 66, 87, 107, 109, 110, 111, 112, 115, 119, 124, 216, 229
Gospel Arc, 1, 3, 5, 6, 7, 14, 15, 19, 23, 27, 31, 36, 38, 41, 42, 44, 46, 48, 50, 51, 52, 54, 56, 57, 58, 59, 60, 63, 64, 66, 67, 69, 71, 73, 74, 76, 79, 81, 82, 83, 86, 89, 91, 93, 95, 97, 99, 101, 103, 105, 106, 107, 109, 110, 112, 113, 115, 119, 123, 124, 125, 126, 128, 131, 133, 135, 136, 138, 140, 141, 143, 146, 150, 154, 158, 163, 166, 169, 171, 174, 178, 182, 185, 188, 192, 195, 198, 200, 204, 205, 207, 210, 212, 213, 215, 216, 220, 222, 223, 224, 225, 228, 230, 234
gospel thread tool, 65, 107, 228
grace, 88, 121, 123

hermeneutic
  rationalistic, 38, 168
history
  redemptive, 193, 195
Holy Spirit, 10, 12, 14, 23, 27, 31, 33, 46, 52, 54, 60, 74, 75, 85, 94, 97, 98, 133, 134, 146, 152, 156, 175, 176, 178, 180, 188, 222, 226
  mysterious movements, 17
human condition
  universal, 27, 60, 65, 94, 97, 98, 107, 110, 125, 131, 146, 158, 170, 226, 228
human condition, 60, 93, 94, 96, 105, 136, 138, 225, 226

identity
  grace-based, 20
  Jesus, 20
  race, 20, 23, 236, 237
  works-based, 20
imperative, 183
incarnation, 50, 146, 217
indicative, 183
interpretive key
  to Scripture, 42
interpretive tool, 59, 82, 224

justification
  functional, 20
  functional identity, 21
  Jesus, 23, 25, 91, 152
  legal source, 146
  of our being, 19
  sanctification, 21, 23, 29, 31, 91, 97, 148, 150, 152, 154, 156, 157, 158, 164, 166, 171, 173, 174, 175, 176, 178, 180, 181, 182, 183, 215, 220, 221
  self, 21, 31, 91, 98

law

SUBJECT INDEX

and gospel, 152, 154, 169, 173, 178, 180, 183, 185
inability, 170
in sanctification, 176
Judaism, 19
over-concern for, 176
role, 174
spectacular function of, 183
spiritually progressive, 19
that which demands, 169
third use, 178
traditional, 19, 46
life
    Spirit-filled, 157
life change
    Antinomian, 150, 158
    gospel, 150, 156, 158
    moralistic, 150, 158
    mystery of, 150
    self-activating, 152
listen
    for others, 58, 74, 77, 80, 223
    for yourself, 57, 74, 75, 79, 223
    to the World of the Text, 58, 74, 76, 79, 223
listening tool, 58, 74, 224
literalism
    wooden, 38
literary tool, 63, 95, 227
literature
    apocalyptic, 63, 83, 96, 103, 228
    narrative, 63, 83, 95, 101, 227
    poetic, 63, 83, 96, 103, 228
    propositional, 63, 83, 95, 101, 227
    wisdom, 63, 83, 95, 101, 227
lost lover, 125, 126

meaning
    original historical, 50, 81, 89, 93, 103, 110, 117, 118, 125, 190, 193, 195, 197, 198, 202, 205, 212, 213, 214, 215, 216
    surplus of, 48, 65, 66, 107, 109, 110, 119, 121, 124, 202, 205, 212, 228, 229
moralism, 36
moralistic preaching, 36, 39
movement

1, 139
2, 139, 140
3, 139, 140
4, 140
mystery, 125, 155, 159
mysticism, 73, 145

natures
    flesh and spirit, 154

Pelagianism, 42
Pole 1, 48, 50, 51, 52, 65, 66, 81, 93, 103, 105, 107, 109, 110, 117, 119, 124, 125, 126, 127, 128, 205, 212, 215, 216, 228, 229, 230
Pole 2, 48, 50, 51, 52, 66, 106, 107, 109, 110, 117, 119, 123, 124, 125, 126, 127, 128, 205, 212, 215, 229, 230
power
    biblical-theological, 56, 141
    dynamic, 146, 148, 171, 178
    legal, 146, 148, 171
    of God, 25, 27, 41, 54, 158, 174, 180, 205
    verbal, 162, 221, 222
Poythress, 190, 191
    Vern, 190
prayer, 55, 75, 89, 150, 239
preaching
    biblical, 38
    Christiconic, 36, 37
    Christocentric, 36, 54, 111, 120
    moralistic, 34, 38
    obsession with, 12
preparing
    crafting, 14
principle
    ethical, 63, 83, 95, 101, 227
proclaiming
    delivering, 14
prophets, 200, 202, 208, 212

racism
    Peter's, 21, 25
read backwards, 52, 66, 109, 110, 229
read forward, 52, 65, 107, 110, 228

reading
  bi-directional, 216
reason, 21, 77, 98, 168, 192, 204
  devotion to, 38
Reformation, 42
reign
  present, 50, 146, 217
renewal
  biblical, 154
repentance
  salvation strategy, 25
revelation
  displaces, 38
righteousness
  ever-elusive, 19, 21
  functional, 21
  received, 21, 90, 146, 239
  self-attained, 21
running commentary, 59, 82, 85, 86, 89, 224

saint
  split-, 33
salvation
  comprehensive, 13, 42, 54, 91, 138, 158, 163, 171, 219
  grace, 21
  pattern of significance, 216
  self-, 25, 27, 31, 34, 36, 42, 61, 91, 94, 97, 171, 174, 183, 226
  works, 21
sanctification
  activating, 23
  present, 29
  self-, 23, 25, 31
savior
  functional, 21, 27
school
  of experience, 10, 14
self
  Adamic, 27
  conflicted, 29, 31, 154, 156, 158, 174
  continuous spiritual-, 154, 156
  divided, 29
  new, 29, 148, 154
  Spirit, 29
  split, 29
  zombie, 29, 177
self-improvement, 12
sermon map, 69, 103, 129, 131, 133, 135, 136, 139, 231, 232, 233, 234, 235
sermon message
  craft a, 67, 69, 129, 230, 231
  Tool 1, 67, 129, 231
  Tool 2, 69, 129, 231
serpent
  bronze, 114, 115, 116, 193
sin
  dark powers of, 23
  in the singular, 27
  nature of, 27, 29
  original, 27
sixth sense, 50, 54
speech-act, 61, 94, 95, 99, 100, 101, 102, 117, 226, 227
spiritual
  success, 27
  techniques, 12, 27
sticky statement, 60, 61, 66, 67, 69, 93, 94, 95, 96, 109, 112, 124, 125, 128, 129, 131, 133, 136, 226, 227, 230, 231

Ten Commandments, 113
textual map, 59, 81, 82, 83, 85, 89, 224
third word, 152, 178, 180, 182
tomb, 29, 148, 170, 171, 173, 176, 183, 204
two words
  of God, 154

veil
  existential, 214
  hermeneutical, 213
victory
  comprehensive, 41
  the King's, 41
view
  allegorical, 117, 186, 188
  evangelical, 118, 162, 186, 188
  liberal, 117, 186
vivid image, 125

Name Index

Abraham, 36, 87, 194, 208

Barnett, Paul, 214
Bauckham, Richard, 163
Bock, Darrell, 190
Bruner, Frederick, 199
Burridge, Richard, 207

Caleb, 113
Cleopas, 199

David, 27, 87, 115, 123, 186, 188, 199, 205, 238

France, R. T., 199

Goldsworthy, Graeme, 164
Goliath, 87, 115

Hannah, John, 7, 9, 10, 14
Horton, Mike, 25

Isaac, 87

Jesus
    death and resurrection, 28
    experience, 14, 25, 27, 29, 31, 46, 54, 69, 75, 107, 131, 135, 138, 164, 220, 221, 222, 233
    his salvation, 7, 9, 12, 14, 19, 21, 23, 25, 27, 29, 31, 33, 34, 41, 46, 48, 50, 54, 66, 73, 74, 87, 101, 104, 109, 110, 112, 113, 114, 115, 117, 119, 121, 122, 123, 124, 125, 127, 131, 135, 138, 145, 148, 150, 154, 156, 158, 164, 171, 174, 180, 181, 183, 205, 217, 220, 221, 222, 229
    leaving behind, 17, 19
    my force, 9
    Pelagian, 12
    plus, 27, 152, 158
    rear-view mirror, 10
    systematic, 12
    textual, 5, 12, 46, 50, 52, 54, 56, 63, 66, 67, 87, 104, 106, 107, 109, 117, 124, 125, 126, 127, 128, 129, 131, 133, 135, 136, 139, 140, 186, 228, 230, 231
    UFO, 12
    ultimate friend, 10
Jonah, 119, 121, 199
Joshua, 113

Kaiser, Walter, 190
Keller, Timothy, 33, 40, 77, 98
Kuruvilla, Abraham, 36

Leithart, Peter, 166
Lindbeck, George, 38, 42
Lovelace, Richard, 31

NAME INDEX

Luther, Martin, 25, 31, 41, 99, 153, 158, 159, 175

Marshall, Walter, 152
Meyer, Lodewijk, 168
Moses, 87, 112, 114, 115, 116, 188, 193, 200, 202, 204, 205, 207, 212, 213, 214, 215

Nathan, 87

Payne, Philip, 190, 193
Pharaoh, 87

Saul, 90, 115, 123, 236

Ward, Timothy, 16

Scripture Index

Genesis
1:3	166
3	17, 36, 116, 150
3.15	200

Leviticus
18:21, 20:2–5	90

Numbers
14:9	115
21:4–9	116
13	114
21	198

1 Samuel
16	117
17	117
17:52	117
27–31	125
30	125
30:1	125

2 Samuel
12:7	88

1 Kings
11:7, 23:10	90

Psalms
19	152
23:1	116
29:5	8, 166

Song of Songs
3:1–5	129, 130
3:5	127

Matthew
1:23	115
4:8	212
5	187
5:17	212
5:48	173
16:24	25
23:27	181

Mark
4:21–5	216
4:31–35	121
4:38	123
4:41	123
8:34	25

Luke
2:41–51	17
3:4–6	216
4:1–13	170

Luke (continued)

7:1–10	84, 121
9:23	25
10:29	99
10:40	100
10.41	100
15	154, 156, 157
24	51, 74
24:25	207
24:25–7	205
24:44–46	221

John

1:1–3	218
1:14	218
1:14–18	114
1:18	114
1:45	218
3:14	117
3:5–7	183
5:39–40	45–7, 209
5:39–47	204, 210, 218, 220
5:45	210
6:29	164
6:68	175
10:14–15	116
14:6	183
15	164
16:12–15	197
17:3	154

Acts

13:15; 17:2–3	221
15	22

Romans

1–2	187
1:16	41, 53, 162, 170, 179, 227, 231
1:16–17	26
1:18–32	152
10	164
10:14–17	40
10:17	41
12:1–2	170
4:25	177
5:1	177
5–8	27
6:1–11	176
6:6	152
6–8	158
7	29, 174, 188
7:1–6	38
7:24	29
7:6	183
7:7–13	179
7.14–25	29
7–8	29
8:1–2	175, 176, 177
8:3	177
8:5	183
8:15	27
8:15–17	175
9	119
10:1–4	121, 131, 142
5	174
5:18	152
6:11–14, 7:1–6	158
8:1–4	150

1 Corinthians

1–2	100
2:2	220, 222, 228, 229
15:3–4	229
15:4	125

2 Corinthians

3:7	174
3:7	9, 222
3:9	7, 220
3:10	222
3:14	221
3:14–16	221
3:15	221
3:16–17	222
3:17–18	222
12:9	125

Galatians

1:2	100
1:6	21, 25
2	12, 23

2:11–14	25	1:5–6	231
2:13	23	1:5–7	41, 162
2:14	25	1:6	164
2:20	160	1:13	175
2:21	177	1:15	114
3, 175	188	2:11–15	115
3:3	175	3:9–10	180
3–4	42	3:10	180
3:1–3	42	4:3–4	78
3:1–6	156, 164, 181		
3:1–7	158		

1 Timothy

1:8–9	185

3:16–22	41		
3:19–26	179		
3:28	23		

2 Timothy

4:9	27, 38		
5	29, 158, 160	3:16	197
5:1	175, 177		
5:6	164		

Hebrews

1:1	207
4:12	167
12:1–2	139

Ephesians

3:20–21	177
4:22	158
4–6	158
5:18	160
5:5	183
6	160

1 Peter

1:23	41

2 Peter

1:20–21	197

Philippians

2:5	170
2:12	164

1 John

4:18	152, 175

Colossians

1	139, 164

www.ingramcontent.com/pod-product-compliance
Lightning Source LLC
Chambersburg PA
CBHW071232170426
43191CB00032B/1324